M000210794

TWELVE WHAT ABOUTS

John Samson is an ordained minister, Reformed pastor, author and Conference speaker, with a passion for the local Church and for the free offer of the gospel to be proclaimed far and wide. He serves as the pastor of King's Church in Phoenix, Arizona. He is a contributing writer at www.reformationtheology.com and maintains his own internet blog at www.effectualgrace.com.

TWELVE WHAT ABOUTS

Answering Common Objections Concerning
God's Sovereignty in Election

John Samson

SOLID GROUND CHRISTIAN BOOKS
BIRMINGHAM, ALABAMA USA

Solid Ground Christian Books
PO Box 660132
Vestavia Hills AL 35266
205-443-0311
www.solid-ground-books.com
mike.sgcb@gmail.com

TWELVE WHAT ABOUTS:
Answering Common Objections Concerning God's Sovereignty in Election

by John Samson

First Solid Ground edition, February 2012

Unless otherwise indentified, all Scripture quotations are from *The Holy Bible, English Standard Version (ESV)*, copyright © 2001 by Crossway Bibles, a division of Good News Publishers. Used by permission. All rights reserved. Other versions include: the Holy Bible, New International Version® (NIV®). Copyright © 1973, 1978, 1984 by International Bible Society, www.ibs.org. All rights reserved worldwide; the New American Standard Bible®, (NASB), Copyright © 1960, 1962, 1963, 1968, 1971, 1972, 1973, 1975, 1977, 1995 by The Lockman Foundation Used by permission (www.Lockman.org); and the King James Version (KJV).

Cover design by Jules LaPierre

© 2012 John F. M. Samson

All rights reserved. No part of this publication may be reproduced or distributed in any form or by any means, or stored in a database or retrieval system, without prior written permission.

ISBN: 978-1-59925-276-6

In honor of

My father
Rev. Redvers J. Samson
1917-2005

Powerful Evangelist, Passionately Reformed

My mother
Muriel Grace Samson
1926 –

Your faithful devotion to God in both good and hard times is
the hallmark of your life. God continues to use you greatly and I
am very proud to be your loving son.

Contents

FOREWORD

John Hendryx

I want to commend, to all readers seeking an honest look into these matters, this very fine treatment in which Pastor Samson carefully answers the most common objections to the biblical doctrine of divine election.

I have known John for many years now and have had the honor to labor alongside him on our blog at **reformationtheology.com** since October, 2005. Though we have never met in person, I know him to be a man of integrity and one who takes special care that every theological assertion he makes is grounded in the Scripture in its proper context. While even John acknowledges that traditions can be good, I have witnessed John's humility first hand in his willingness to ever evaluate his beliefs in the light of the text of Scripture.

Along with true believers from every age, Pastor Samson affirms that God commands all people everywhere to repent and believe the gospel and that every person who does so will be saved. Christ will never fail to keep His promise to receive all people who come to Him. He also affirms that every man who responds to the gospel call does so because he desires to do so. To be saved we must all personally and willingly trust Him. These statements can all be found among the promises of the Bible. But the same Bible that affirms that all people must repent and believe in Jesus in order to be saved also unequivocally declares that all people, because they are born in bondage to sin, are utterly impotent to repent and believe.

Rejecting and receiving Jesus Christ as Lord and Savior is not a passive non-moral act, but a deliberate willful moral choice. We choose that which we love. The one who rejects Christ deliberately chooses to say "No" to Christ and "Yes" to self and sin. Likewise, the one who receives Christ says "Yes" to Christ and "no" to sin and self.

John 3:19-20 states that natural men love darkness and will not come into the light. Left to themselves men will always choose to stay in darkness. Whether or not someone believes or rejects Christ, it depends completely on the disposition of the heart. Apart from a supernatural work of the Holy Spirit, the Bible says our disposition is, by nature, hostile to God and we cannot understand spiritual truth (Rom. 8:7 & 1 Cor. 2:14). But thanks be to God, the new birth or regeneration, is where God, the Holy Spirit applies the redemptive blessings of Christ, which give us the spiritual life that empowers us to do what we must do (repent and believe the gospel), but cannot do (while in the flesh), because of our bondage to sin (John 6:63, 65).

Clear and plain as the words of Christ regarding His identity may now seem to be, it is important to consider that there was a time when even Jesus' disciples (who spent 3 years with him) did not understand them. Seeing they did not see, and hearing they did not hear (Matt. 13:13). They could not comprehend that the Messiah was to be "cut off" (Isa. 53:8). They refused to receive the teaching that their own Rabbi must die. Therefore, when He was finally crucified ... when the Shepherd was finally struck down ... they were confounded and His sheep were scattered each to his own way. Although Jesus had often told them of it, they had never internalized it as a fact. They were blinded to it.

Let us watch and pray to God against such prejudice in our own heart. Let us beware of allowing traditions, preconceived notions and unaided logic to take root in our hearts and blind us to Jesus. There is only one test of truth: what the Scripture says. Before this all the prejudices in our hearts must fall.

But even the disciples who read the Scripture still did not understand. And when they finally did, what was it that made the difference? How did they finally see Jesus for who He was? In Matthew chapter 16:13-17 Jesus asked His disciples the most important question they were ever asked. Jesus asked, "...who do you say that I am?" Simon Peter replied, "You are the Christ, the Son of the living God." And Jesus answered him, "Blessed are

10

you, Simon Bar-Jonah, for flesh and blood has not revealed this to you, but my Father who is in heaven."

Notice that the first thing Jesus wants to make certain Peter understands when making his declaration is that this mystery cannot be truly known by human reason, but only by God's revelation through the Holy Spirit (1 Cor. 12:3; Matt. 11:25-27). "Flesh and blood" simply refers to the natural resources of man without the Holy Spirit.

Left to himself with his natural depravity blinding him, Peter would never have understood the truth, beauty and excellence of Christ and His true identity. Left to himself, Simon wouldn't have marveled at Jesus as the Son of God, the Savior of the world. But God Himself had revealed this truth to him by giving him a new heart (Ezek. 36:26) in which the Spirit cries ABBA FATHER (Rom. 8:14-17), and so his eyes were opened for the first time to recognize who Jesus really is. Apart from the Spirit of God there is no understanding of Spiritual truth (1 Cor. 2:10-14) even when it is staring you in the face. You may intellectually understand what the words mean, but the heart is so naturally prejudiced against Christ, that the Spirit must disarm those hostilities if we are to see the truth in them.

Apart from a new heart, the problem in our natural state is that we are all spiritually blind (not merely short-sighted). 2 Corinthians 4:3-4 says: "If our gospel is veiled, it is veiled to those who are perishing, whose minds the god of this age has blinded, who do not believe, lest the light of the gospel of the glory of Christ, who is the image of God, should shine on them." So if God does not open our spiritual eyes, we will never be able to recognize Jesus. Unless God intervenes to replace our eyes, we are, like the disciples, incapable of recognizing Christ as He really is.

In the flesh we can go listen to a preacher, we can read the Bible, yet unless God reveals Himself directly to us, we are dead to spiritual truth (Eph. 2:1). While reading the text we will actually fail to recognize Him, just as the disciples on the road to Emmaus, until Jesus opened their eyes. And that is why we need God to intervene, to take away our spiritual blindness, so that we can see clearly what otherwise is beyond our natural resources to comprehend.

11

It seems that Jesus believes it is critical to remind Peter of this truth as of first importance in Peter's "follow-up". Many in this day and age are reluctant to speak to a new Christian about God's sovereign grace in salvation for fear it is a hard truth. Yet when Peter makes his first confession of Christ, Jesus puts it first before all other truths.

Because He does not want to leave any room for Peter to attribute his understanding to his own wisdom, prudence, sound judgment, or good sense, providing no room whatsoever for boasting. He wants, rather, to turn Peter's eyes toward God as the Author of his salvation from eternity in Christ (Eph. 1:3-5). Salvation from first to last is of the Lord. Jesus not only justifies us when we come to faith, but raised us, when dead in sin, that we may indeed have faith.

I can just hear some cry out, "That's not fair!"

Well, for God to be unfair, we can all be thankful. If God operated solely on the basis of fairness there would not be a single person alive and reading this today, since we all are deserving of His wrath.

It is the author's purpose to answer these kinds of objections to the biblical doctrine of election. As you will see, his answers are drawn from the text of Scripture, not his own ideas or theories. He reminds us that grace is freely given and not dependent on our meeting certain conditions. That grace is not a reward for our faith but the very cause of it.

So again I want to commend this fine work by Pastor Samson on the topic of God's sovereign grace. John is one of the most passionate Christians I know, whose number one purpose is to make Christ known. This work on the doctrine of election is no exception. In it you will find that the purpose of election is to bring all glory to Jesus Christ in our salvation.

John Hendryx
monergism.com, January, 2012

A WORD TO THE READER

Question: WHY THIS BOOK?

Answer: For the glory of God.

Question: FOR WHOM IS THIS BOOK WRITTEN?

Answer: Christians who believe the Bible is the word of God and who wish to gain a biblical understanding of God's electing grace in Christ.

Question: WHO WILL GAIN MOST FROM THE BOOK?

Answer: Those who are willing to test and examine their traditions and hold them up to the light of Scripture, the sole infallible rule of faith for the people of God.

This is not an easy process at times, more for emotional rather than intellectual reasons. Many of us have been told things by highly respected people in our lives (such as the person who led us to Christ, or a revered pastor or Bible teacher, or a father or mother in the faith) that, upon analysis, may not in fact be true. Sometimes, to actually test such statements can feel like an act of betrayal on our part. Yet, it is vital for all who desire to be led by the Spirit of truth to yield to His leading rather than maintain an emotional allegiance to what many call "theological love lines."

A WORD ABOUT BIBLE INTERPRETATION

Hermeneutics is the science of biblical interpretation. One amongst many sound principles of interpretation is that we should build all doctrine on necessary rather than possible inferences.

13

A necessary inference is something that is definitely taught by the text. The conclusion is unavoidable. It is necessary.

A possible inference is something that could or might be true, but not something actually stated by the text. Some refer to this as the distinction between the implicit and the explicit.

An implication may be drawn from the text of Scripture, but we then have to ask if the implicit interpretation is a NECESSARY ONE rather than a POSSIBLE one. We all have our theories, but a sound principle we should employ is to not believe or teach as doctrine something that is only a possible interpretation. We should build doctrine ONLY on necessary interpretation.

In practical terms, making these distinctions can sometimes be a difficult process because it means we have to take a step back and thoroughly analyze exactly why we think a verse or passage teaches something. In other words, it means testing our traditions and doing a lot of thinking. Yet this is something we should do constantly.

THINK OVER WHAT I SAY

Paul exhorted Timothy to "Think over what I say, for the Lord will give you understanding in everything." (2 Tim. 2:7)

All of us should be prepared to hold up our preconceived notions to the light of Scripture to see if these assumptions are valid or not. The result of this process often involves the killing of some sacred cows; but that's a good thing, if what we have held to be true cannot actually be supported by the biblical text. We all have our blind spots and traditions, but we are not always aware of them. Therefore, the serious Bible student asks questions of the text constantly in order to determine what the sacred text actually says and then builds all thinking and doctrine on that.

Here's one text as an example: John 20:19 says, "On the evening of that day, the first day of the week, the doors being locked where the disciples were for fear of the Jews, Jesus came and stood among them and said to them, 'Peace be with you.'"

Many people read this passage and conclude that Jesus walked through the locked door in order to present Himself to His disciples.

But does the text actually say that? No, it does not. The text MIGHT be teaching that. It is certainly a possible inference drawn from the text, but by no means a necessary one. There are other possible explanations.

Concerning this verse the ESV Study Bible says (correctly in my opinion), *Some interpreters understand the doors being locked to imply that Jesus miraculously passed through the door or the walls of the room, though the text does not explicitly say this. Since Jesus clearly had a real physical body with flesh and bones after he rose from the dead... one possibility is that the door was miraculously opened so that the physical body of Jesus could enter, which is consistent with the passage about Peter going through a locked door some time later (see Acts 12:10).*

To state the principle again: we should build all doctrine on necessary rather than possible inferences, on the explicit and not the implicit. All else is speculation.

Another sound rule of Bible interpretation is that we should interpret the unclear passages in Scripture in light of the clear. Though all Scripture is God-breathed, not every passage is equally clear (easy to understand). Even the Apostle Peter struggled with Paul's writings at times, as he found some of it "hard to understand, which the untaught and unstable distort, as they do also the rest of the Scriptures, to their own destruction." (2 Pet. 3:16).

When determining what the Bible teaches on a particular topic, we should find the passages which CLEARLY address the issue at hand and make them the starting point of our doctrine, rather than an obscure (or less than clear) passage. Once that which is clear is firmly grasped and understood, then we should proceed to study the passages that at first seem unclear, using the other interpretive rules.

These distinctions I make are not mine in terms of origin. They are carefully thought-out methods or rules of interpretation employed by all sound teachers of the Bible. Of course, none of us follow our own interpretive rules consistently, which is why Christians and even scholars make mistakes, and why, even with the exact same Bible in front of us, we do not all see things the same way. We ALL have our blind spots and traditions.

One more thing: If there is a contradiction between two views, at least one of them is wrong. God is not confused even if we are. He is not the author of confusion. Our task as students of the Bible and disciples of Christ is to search out the Scriptures to find out what they actually teach.

HOW MUCH DO YOU WANT IT?

The opening verses of Proverbs 2 say:

1 My son, if you receive my words and treasure up my commandments with you,
2 making your ear attentive to wisdom and inclining your heart to understanding;
3 yes, if you call out for insight and raise your voice for understanding,
4 if you seek it like silver and search for it as for hidden treasures,
5 then you will understand the fear of the LORD and find the knowledge of God.
6 For the LORD gives wisdom; from his mouth come knowledge and understanding...

The promises of verses 5 and 6 are conditional upon heeding the requirements set forth in verses 1 through 4.

When God opens our eyes to see the beauty of Christ and His gospel, it is entirely His work. He opens our blind eyes to give us the miracle of spiritual sight. Yet once we are disciples of Christ, spiritual growth is not automatic. For this growth to happen, we have to pursue God, asking Him to open up our understanding, while searching out the Scriptures. This is not to be some half-hearted attempt at spiritual progress. Indeed, this is no trivial pursuit. God rewards those who diligently seek Him. (Heb 11:6)

Note the requirements listed here in Proverbs 2:1-6: we are told to receive and treasure God's word, make the ear attentive, incline the heart, call out for insight, raise the voice for understanding, seek it like silver, search for it as for hidden treasures... THEN (for those who fulfill these conditions) the promise is made that God will bring understanding of the fear and knowledge of Himself. He will give us His wisdom, knowledge and understanding. I trust that this is your strong desire.

The words of these verses have been used as a prayer of mine over a number of decades now and I hope you, the reader, will make it your prayer too as we take this journey into the Scriptures. The phrase "mouth of God" in verse 6, is a clear reference to the Scriptures. This is how we are called to live, not by bread alone, but "by every word that comes from the mouth of God." (Matt. 4:4).

May each of us be led by the Holy Spirit, knowing that as we continue in His word, we shall be seen to be His true disciples, experiencing the reality of Jesus' promise that "you will know the truth, and the truth will set you free" (John 8:31, 32).

Question: WHY SHOULD ANYONE BE INTERESTED IN THIS SUBJECT?

Answer: Firstly, Divine election is a theme mentioned often in sacred Scripture. God has chosen to reveal this truth for the spiritual nurture and growth of the people of God. Obviously, it is something He wishes us to know.

Secondly, rightly understood, the doctrine of unconditional election (God's choice in the salvation of sinners being based on no human merit whatsoever) removes all possible ground for boasting and establishes the Gospel message of grace.

Question: WHAT IS THE PURPOSE OF THIS BOOK?

Answer: That each Christian who reads it will enjoy more of their blessed inheritance in Christ, knowing the Father's love, grace and mercy in ways they might never have known before.

Interested?

If so, then please read on...

CHAPTER 1

THE PLACE TO START—
AMAZED BY COMMON GRACE

Common Grace. It is a term used in theology to describe the grace God gives to every living person on planet earth. It is called "common," not because it is not worth that much, but because everyone alive gets it.

Grace by definition can never be demanded. God gives grace, not because He has to, but because He decides to. The Scripture says that God "makes his sun rise on the evil and on the good, and sends rain on the just and on the unjust." (Matt. 5:45).

How gracious this is of God. God doesn't discriminate against the non-Christian in sending His rain, but gives it freely to saint and sinner alike. That should amaze us. It should take our breath away in fact. Yet the concept of common grace doesn't usually do that for us. We're very much accustomed to it, because it is so common. But we must always remember that God is exceedingly gracious in dispensing this kind of grace on people. The point being, He in no way has to.

Through the use of a short story, I'd like to give you a glimpse into why common grace should amaze us.

The story concerns a young Christian lady of 18 years of age in York, England. Born in Malta, of Irish parents, she was engaged to be married to a bright young man in the British military. The plan was that after the war was over, they would both serve the Lord as missionaries together, wherever He would lead them to go.

Sent over to France on D-Day, June 6, 1944, the young man was thrust into the battle for the city of Caen in Normandy, France. Tragically, just weeks afterward, on July 10, 1944, he was killed by one of the enemies' bullets.

On hearing the news of her fiancé's death, the young lady was obviously devastated. Grief filled her heart. While attending church services in York for the next several months, she would hear dramatic testimonies of Divine protection, as loved ones returned home recounting the stories. All of these returning soldiers were protected from imminent danger. Many of these soldiers were extremely conscious of the Lord's direct intervention in keeping them alive. And yet, the young lady had to live on knowing that the man she loved was not coming home.

Question after question plagued the young lady's mind. Nothing that was said to her seemed to ease the pain and grief. And those hostile, haunting questions continued relentlessly.

One day, she rushed into her bedroom and flung herself down on the bed in great grief, as she often did. Then something very dramatic and life-changing happened. The Lord Himself appeared to this young lady. The brightness of His glory filled the room. He didn't say a word. But in that moment, He stretched out His hand to her. She was totally caught up with the look in His eyes. She beheld the greatest love and compassion in the world. All her questions subsided as He smiled at her. Her heart's cry was answered by one look into His eyes, full of unspeakable love.

The young lady very rarely speaks of this incident. However, when she does, usually only with close family and friends, tears well up once again at the grace she found in the face of Christ.

The story continues. At the same time, a Welsh military man was stationed in the same city of York in England. Brought up as a Roman Catholic, this young man had a dramatic conversion to Christ while serving in the British army in Gibraltar. In understanding the Gospel of Christ, this young man came out of the Roman Catholic Church system, facing the hostility of his family in doing so, and then trained to serve the British forces as a military chaplain.

Very much an Evangelist, this young man saw countless men come to Christ while serving in France and Belgium. For an eighteen month period, the numbers of soldiers he saw professing faith in Christ numbered in the hundreds every week.

One day, this young man was preaching in the city of York, and his eyes fixed on a certain young lady - the lady in our story. The two began to court each other and married soon after.

Years of married life passed and the hope of having a child grew stronger and stronger. How they wanted a child! Yet time was marching on.

Seventeen years of marriage came and went and no child was forthcoming. Just when it looked like all hope was gone, the young lady became pregnant. What joy must have filled the home with this dramatic news!

Two weeks before due date, the baby was coming. Complications ensued, with the afterbirth coming first, and the mother losing a great deal of blood. The mother was not doing at all well and the little baby was fighting for its life. Once born, the little one was whisked away into an oxygen tent where every gasping breath was a severe struggle.

Years later, the father wrote the following words: "I remember when I was called to the hospital where my son lay near to death. When he saw me, he reached out desperately towards me. I could do nothing. He was in an oxygen tent. The doctor gave me a knowing and sympathizing look and shook her head. The lad was dying."

He continued, "I found a corner where I prayed. I thanked God for the joy that boy had brought into my life, for the privilege of having responsibility for his welfare, be it but for a short while. I told God how much that child meant to me and added, 'but really he belonged to You all the time. Lord I commend him to Your safe keeping. He means more than life to me Lord, but though You take him, I'll love You still and will praise You all my days.' That, I learned many years later, was a sacrifice of praise."

Both the mother and the young child survived and in fact the child grew to be a robust baby boy and gained all his babyhood milestones early. Then at age 13 months he began to develop a cough, which became persistent. The doctor diagnosed it as croup.

Every night between 8 pm and 9 pm, and 11 pm and midnight, and 4 am and 5 am, the boy would cough with every breath he took. The mother tried medicine and hot drinks each time, hoping for some measure of relief for the child, while the whole household tried to catch some sleep until the next coughing bout began. As you might imagine, the parents faced their busy work schedule the next day after having had a very disturbed night of sleep.

The problem became more and more pronounced so that every night was punctuated by 3 hours of perpetual coughing with permanently disturbed sleep. This went on each night for 4 years.

Every Fall, the boy was rushed to hospital to be in an oxygen tent to recover from these severe breathing and coughing bouts. On his return home, the parents had to keep an electric kettle boiling in his bedroom all night to help with these croup attacks.

From September until May (from age 3 to age 7) the boy was not allowed to play outside and his mother had to invent paper and pencil games to keep him amused. At age 4 he had surgery to have his tonsils removed to see if that would help the situation but there was no respite until age 7 when continual prayer was answered and the attacks stopped.

The neighborhood boys were all older than he and so when he was 8 years old he was allowed to run after and fetch the soccer ball to help with the game. This must have inspired the boy because he soon made the school soccer team, later to the city of Chester schoolboy's team, and at age 14 and 15 he was top scorer. He once scored 9 goals in a single game and his coaches were seeking to help him become a professional soccer player.

The Lord had a different path for him though. Today he serves the Lord as a minister of the Gospel. I am sure you will agree that he is a trophy of God's grace.

Why do I tell you all this?

Well, let me give you the names of the two parents in the story. The lady's name is Muriel Grace Macnamara. The man's name is Rev. Redvers Joseph Samson. The lady is my mother and the man is my father. Therefore, their story is really my story too.

I was the young baby fighting for life, the young child with such health issues that just helping my Dad clear snow from the home driveway meant being rushed to the hospital with double pneumonia; and the same young man who grew to be something of a soccer player before the Lord intervened to send him in a different direction. I am very conscious that I am alive because of the gracious hand of God upon my life. Every breath I take is a gift of Divine grace.

I am overwhelmed when I think of God, in His grace, allowing so many of His enemies to continue to breathe His air and see the splendors of His creation, each and every day, as they enjoy His sunlight and the benefits of His rain. How gracious God truly is.

The Lord is good to all. He is the giver of all life and even sustains the lives of both Gospel preachers and terrorists alike. The Scripture says, "Since he himself gives to all mankind life and breath and everything... for 'In him we live and move and have our being.'" (Acts 17:25, 28).

The fact that you are reading this right now tells me that God has been unspeakably good to you. The old hymn says, "Count your blessings, name them one by one, and it will surprise you what the Lord has done."

As you take the time to think about God's blessings on your life, I trust that you will therefore, like me, stand amazed by common grace. You and I are living, breathing and moving because of the wonderful grace of God. It is therefore not to be thought of lightly. Common Grace is a designation made by theologians and speaks of the commonality of grace only in contrast to that which is special. In common grace, God gives life and health, sun and rain to those who don't deserve it. In special electing grace, God chooses to intervene in the lives of some (but not all) who are already experiencing common grace, and speaks life into the deadness of human hearts, causing them to be raised from spiritual death (to be born again).

And it is to this theme—God's special electing grace—that the rest of the book now turns, both in its proclamation, and its defense.

CHAPTER 2

THE WIND BLOWS WHERE IT WISHES

In the early verses of John chapter 3, Jesus tells Nicodemus in no uncertain terms, the absolute necessity of being born again (or born from above). Unless a man is first born again (regenerated, made alive spiritually) he can never enter or even see the kingdom of God. Jesus stresses the fact that this new birth is not merely an optional extra. It is imperative. Jesus said, "You must be born again." (3:7)

Jesus didn't tell Nicodemus what he must do to be born again. That is because it was not within Nicodemus' power to perform this miracle. "That which is born of the flesh is flesh, and that which is born of the Spirit is spirit." (John 3:6) Flesh can only reproduce flesh. It takes the Spirit to regenerate the human spirit. This miracle of regeneration cannot be achieved by human effort or by self-performed surgery.

The new birth is not the improvement of the old nature, but the creation of an entirely new one. It is a birth, a new birth, and like the first one we experienced, it did not occur because of our decision to be born. Our will was not a factor in any way. We were born as a result of the will of others—that of our parents, and of course, God's will to create us using the means of human, physical intimacy.

In contrast to our first birth, this new birth does not occur through human means. God alone brings about this new creation in Christ Jesus. As John, the Gospel writer had already

d out in chapter 1:12, 13, "But to all who did receive him,
ɔlieved in his name, he gave the right to become children
of God, who were born, not of blood nor of the will of the flesh
nor of the will of man, but of God."

Jesus makes it clear that human flesh can only reproduce flesh.
It is the Holy Spirit alone who can recreate human spirits. The
Holy Spirit is the sole Agent working regeneration in the
human spirit.

In explaining this phenomenon of the new birth, Jesus then
speaks of something very mysterious—the wind. Wind is
mysterious, not because it is not real, but because it is not
something we've ever actually seen. Though we know when it
is around because of its effects, we've never actually observed
wind with our eyes. Oh, we've seen trees swaying, leaves
falling, papers flying through the air. Sometimes the effects of
the wind are so powerful that the only word we can use for its
effects would be "devastation." The wind can cause havoc on a
massive scale, as the victims of hurricanes can testify. But wind
is mysterious because we cannot see it and we are never sure
about where it came from or where it is going. It seems to have
a mind of its own.

Concerning this, Jesus said, "The wind blows where it wishes,
and you hear its sound, but you do not know where it comes
from or where it goes. So it is with everyone who is born of the
Spirit." (John 3:8)

The word *"pneuma"* in Greek, like the word *"ruach"* in Hebrew
means "breath, wind or spirit." Jesus uses an obvious play on
words here, describing the activity of the Holy Spirit in
regeneration.

Of course, much more could and should be said about these
opening verses in John chapter 3. But just for a moment, can we
stop to appreciate the impact of verse 8? Here Jesus teaches us

that when anyone is born of the Spirit, like the blowing of the wind, the invisible Sovereign Spirit of God has moved in mighty power. Yet in contrast to when a town or city experiences storm damage on a large scale, the effects of this "wind" are not in any way negative. Though powerful in the extreme, the Spirit's work is amazingly precise.

When someone is born again, it is evidence of the fact that God the Holy Spirit has performed extensive Divine surgery. He has taken out the stony heart and put in a heart of flesh. Ezekiel 36:26-27 declares, "And I will give you a new heart, and a new spirit I will put within you. And I will remove the heart of stone from your flesh and give you a heart of flesh. And I will put my Spirit within you, and cause you to walk in my statutes and be careful to obey my rules." What an amazing miracle this is!

I remember going to a Christian service at age 14, not wanting to be there, hoping for the service to end (even though it had just begun). I was only there because my father had asked me to go. I had no interest in Christ, nor in what I was observing when the congregation sang, and certainly, I had no interest in what the preacher had to say. But sometime during the message, my attitude changed. I became interested. In fact, I became intrigued. I was fascinated, and struck by the realities of heaven and hell and the need for a Savior. For the first time in my life, I was attracted by a Treasure I had never seen before.

I didn't know it then, but I know now, that what happened in a little metal shed-like building in Chester, England that Sunday night of May 10th, 1980 was this: the Holy Spirit of God, invisibly blew into that service. And while I was hearing the Gospel, in Sovereign and colossal power, yet with the skill of an expert Surgeon, He went to work on my soul. In an instant in time, I was born from above, the old heart of stone was removed and a new heart was put in that with every beat, wanted to know the Master, the Lord Jesus Christ. This Jesus, so to speak, stepped off the old dusty pages of the Bible and became a living Person in my eyes. All of a sudden, I really wanted to know Him, I really wanted Him to save me, and I really wanted His will in my life. And when the Gospel appeal was made, I came to Christ willingly in repentance and faith.

If you are born of the Spirit, God did the exact same thing for you. The Reformation "sola" of "Sola Gratia" (Grace Alone) simply expresses in doctrine what God has done for His people in experience. It is God and God alone who has saved us. All the credit for it goes to Him, because this birth had nothing to do with our intelligence (that we somehow worked out who Jesus was for ourselves), or our humility (we having conquered our own pride, were able to humble ourselves to be able to respond in faith to the Gospel). No, a thousand times, no! We are Christians because of the all conquering power of the mighty Spirit of God, who graciously stormed our hearts and worked His Sovereign will. He brought us forth by the word of truth, causing us to find sheer delight in the presence of God both now and for all eternity.

In John chapter 11, we have the record of Jesus raising Lazarus from the dead. It is interesting to note that after experiencing this mighty resurrection, Lazarus did not immediately seek an attorney in order to sue Jesus for violating his right to stay dead! Nor did all the town's people sue Jesus for failing to raise all of their dead relatives from the graves. No, everyone marveled at the all-powerful call of Jesus. By the power of just His word, He actually brought a putrefying corpse back to life. Of course, no one was more thrilled with this Divine mercy than Lazarus himself.

Why do we speak so much about God's grace? Because, with Lazarus, we can say that by the effectual call of God, grace has conquered our hearts and brought us to life. When we were spiritually dead in our trespasses and sins (the Greek word for dead in Ephesians 2, verses 1 and 5, "*nekros*" means "dead like a corpse") God made us alive (Eph. 2:5).

In Ephesians 2:1-6, we read the Apostle Paul's words to the Christians in Ephesus, "And you were dead in the trespasses and sins in which you once walked, following the course of this world, following the prince of the power of the air, the spirit that is now at work in the sons of disobedience—among whom we all once lived in the passions of our flesh, carrying out the desires of the body and the mind, and were by nature children of wrath, like the rest of mankind. But God, being rich in mercy, because of the great love with which he loved us, even when we were dead in our trespasses, made us alive together with Christ—by grace you have been saved—and raised us up with him and seated us with him in the heavenly places in Christ Jesus..."

To quote the Prince of Preachers, C. H. Spurgeon, *The great King, immortal, invisible, the Divine person, called the Holy Spirit: it is He that stimulates the soul, or else it would lie dead forever; it is He that makes it tender, or else it would never feel; it is He that imparts power to the Word preached, or else it could never reach further than the ear; it is He who breaks the heart, it is He who makes it whole; He, from first to last, is the great worker of Salvation in us, just as Jesus Christ was the author of Salvation for us. (Sermon - Things That Accompany Salvation, found at www.spurgeon.org).*

Amazing grace, how sweet the sound that saved a wretch like me... Twas grace that taught my heart to fear, and grace my fears relieved, how precious did that grace appear, the hour I first believed.

Prayer: "Heavenly Father, Sovereign King, hear our cry. As Your gospel is heralded around the world, may the Holy Spirit of God, like a mighty triumphant wind, conquer dead human hearts today! It is man's only hope! For Your great Name's sake and for Your glory alone. Amen."

CHAPTER 3

A SUPRISING JOURNEY

I was born and raised in Chester, England. My father was a Baptist Evangelist and yet it may be something of a surprise to learn that I never really grew up in church. It would be fair to say our family's home life was a very "Christian" environment, yet because my father used to travel extensively to preach, my mother and I seldom went with him to church services. That was until my dad became the pastor of a local church.

As a child I was extremely bored with the church meetings I did attend and was far more interested in soccer (called "football" over in England). I wanted to be a pro soccer player. My favorite part of the church service was the benediction—I was so glad when it all was over!

I remember seeing my dad reading and studying his Bible (I was probably around age 9 at the time) and thought to myself "that looks so boring to me—spending hours with a book that's hard to read, in language I cannot understand—you'll never catch me doing that."

As I mentioned in the last chapter, one Sunday night, when I was 14, my father did ask me to go with him to hear an evangelist preach. His sermon was on the second coming of Christ. I remember him looking at the crowd, but yet it seemed that his gaze was focused on me, as he said, "For all have sinned and come short of the glory of God." My first thought was, "How does the preacher know of my sin? How does he know I am a sinner?" Like a bolt from the blue I realized my lost condition and that I would be embarrassed with shame if I had to stand before God in that condition.

An appeal was made for salvation and I responded by raising my hand, walking the aisle, signing the card provided... but more than anything I just knew of my need for Christ to be my Savior to hide me from the fierce judgment of God. When I later returned to my seat (after around 15 minutes in a counseling area) my father still had tears streaming down his face. I think it was the first and only time I saw my father cry. Sometime later he told me that both he and my mother had been praying earnestly for my salvation for many years.

I then started attending the church on a regular basis, but as I look back, one of the biggest changes in my life was evident by my new love for Bible study. I would spend all my allowance money on Bible teaching cassette tapes (I know, I am really showing my age when I mention such museum pieces). I just couldn't get enough of the Bible. I would spend 3 – 4 hours every night learning the Scriptures and hearing Bible teaching. That same passionate desire for the Word of God is still present in my life today.

TWO DECADES ON...

Fast forward to November in the year 2000 (more than twenty years after I was converted as a teenager). I had been in full-time ministry since finishing my years of theological training in June of 1987, and was fairly confident that my knowledge of the Word was sound. I was serving as pastor of a church in Phoenix, Arizona.

I received a flyer in the mail from Ligonier Ministries informing me that Dr. R. C. Sproul was coming to do a Friday night and Saturday morning teaching in Scottsdale. That was only a short distance from my home in Phoenix. Up until then, I had not heard Dr. Sproul in person, but had been greatly impacted by his teaching videos on the Holiness of God some years before.

As I looked further at the flyer my heart sank when I saw the subject he was going to be focusing on—"Chosen by God—the biblical doctrines of election and predestination."

Honestly, I thought, "How silly that a man of that caliber would spend his energies articulating an idea so way past its sell-by date." I was in two minds as to whether to go or not. I wanted to hear Dr. Sproul, but not on that subject. Any other subject would have been better as far as I was concerned.

Well, I finally decided to go, but sat on the back row so if it became obvious that Dr. Sproul was just espousing his religious traditions, I could leave quickly and quietly without interrupting folk around me. I was more than prepared for my attendance at the presentation to be a short one.

I stayed for the first session and thought, "Yes, he has a point. I can't fault what he is saying. But I have many Scriptures that would refute his conclusions." However, I was intrigued that there was nothing in what I heard that would be easily dismissed.

Then the conference included a question and answer session on the subject. This proved to be invaluable for me because many of the questions I had were raised, and, I had to admit, were answered from Scripture, in their proper Biblical context.

I was immediately alarmed by this, as I came to understand that this whole issue required a lot more research than I had previously thought. I left the conference unconvinced, but bothered enormously that I had heard no Scripture taken out of context. Being absolutely honest with myself, I had to admit that it was my assumptions about certain texts that were guilty of that exact charge.

Knowing that I needed to believe what Scripture taught on the subject, I ordered much material and began my research. It is never pleasant to examine firmly held traditions, and I felt that this was especially so in my position, when I had taught other things at various times in my ministry. No one wants to admit the possibility that they may in fact have been wrong.

I have to say that it took more than a year of researching the issue in depth before I realized that there was a consistent and clear Biblical doctrine of election and predestination. I also came to see that in order for me to believe what the Bible taught in this area, I had to dispense with my traditional understanding.

I was as surprised as anyone to emerge from this self-imposed theological study cocoon as fully Reformed concerning the doctrines of salvation. Yet that is what happened.

These doctrines can be summarized as follows:

RADICAL CORRUPTION - "The heart is deceitful above all things, and desperately sick; who can understand it?" (Jer. 17:9).

Sinners are completely helpless to redeem themselves or to contribute anything meritorious toward their own salvation. Because of the fall of man, the sinner is not morally neutral, but actually hostile towards God. He is, in fact, the sworn enemy of God. He is spiritually dead, and therefore blind and deaf to the things of God. His will is not free, it is in bondage to his evil nature; therefore, he will not, indeed he cannot choose good over evil. Therefore it takes much more than the Spirit's assistance and wooing to bring a sinner to Christ—it takes a radical regeneration by which the Spirit makes the sinner alive and gives him a new nature—a heart of flesh instead of a heart of stone. Faith is the evidence of the new birth, not the cause of it. Since both repentance and faith are possible only because of the regenerating work of God, both are called the gift of God. (Gen. 2:15-17; Ps. 51:5, Jer. 17:9; John 6:44; 8:34, 47; 10: 26; Rom. 3:10-18, 5:12, 8:7, 8; 1 Cor. 2:14, Eph. 2:1-9; Phil. 1:29; 2 Tim. 2:25; Heb. 12:2; 1 John 5:1)

UNCONDITIONAL ELECTION - "... though they were not yet born and had done nothing either good or bad—in order that God's purpose of election might continue, not because of works but because of him who calls.." (Rom. 9:11).

God's choice of certain individuals unto salvation before the foundation of the world rested solely in His own sovereign will, not being based on any foreseen response or obedience on man's part, such as repentance, faith, etc. On the contrary, God gives faith and repentance to each individual whom He selected. These acts are the result, not the cause of God's choice. Election therefore was not determined by or conditioned upon any virtuous quality or act foreseen in man. God brings His elect, through the power of the Spirit, to a willing acceptance of Christ. Thus God's choice of the sinner, not the sinner's choice of Christ, is the ultimate cause of salvation. (John 1:12, 13; Acts 11:18; 13:48; Rom. 8:28-30; 9:6-21; 1 Cor. 1:30; Eph 1:4-11; 2:1-10)

PARTICULAR REDEMPTION - "...you shall call his name Jesus, for he will save his people from their sins." (Matt. 1:21).

"The death of the Son of God is the only and most perfect sacrifice and satisfaction for sin, and is of infinite worth and value, abundantly sufficient to expiate the sins of the whole world. This death is of such infinite value and dignity because the person who submitted to it was not only really man and perfectly holy, but also the only-begotten Son of God, of the same eternal and infinite essence with the Father and the Holy Spirit, which qualifications were necessary to constitute Him a Savior for us; and, moreover, because it was attended with a sense of the wrath and curse of God due to us for sin." Canons of Dort - Second Head of Doctrine, Articles 3 and 4.

The doctrine of Particular Redemption speaks of God's design in the atonement and who it was He was intending to save when Christ went to the cross. Christ died as a substitute who bore the full weight of God's wrath on behalf of His people, paying the penalty for their sin. Christ intended to save His sheep and actually secured everything necessary for their salvation. The gift of faith is infallibly applied by the Spirit to all for whom Christ died, thereby guaranteeing their salvation. (Isa. 53:5-11; Matt. 1:21; 20:28; Eph. 5:2, 25-27; Tit. 3:5-6, John 10:14-16, 26-30; 17:6-12; Acts 20:28; Rom. 3:21-26; 5:12-21; 8:28-30; Heb. 10:10-14; Rev. 5:9-10; 7:9, 10)

EFFECTUAL CALLING - "...those whom he called he also justified..." (Rom. 8:30).

In addition to the outward general call to salvation which is made to everyone who hears the gospel, the Holy Spirit extends to the elect a special inward call that inevitably brings them to salvation. The external call (which is made to all without distinction) can be, and often is, rejected; whereas the internal call (which is made only to the elect) cannot be rejected. It always results in conversion. By means of this special effectual call, the Spirit irresistibly draws sinners to Christ. He is not limited in His work of applying salvation by man's will, nor is He dependent upon man's cooperation for success. The Spirit graciously causes the elect sinner to cooperate, to believe, to repent, to come freely and willingly to Christ. (Matt. 22:14; 23:37-39; John 1:12-13; 3:1-8; 3:16; 6:44; Rom. 8:28-30; Eph 2:1-6)

PRESERVATION OF THE SAINTS - "...those whom he justified he also glorified." (Rom. 8:30).

God's saving purpose cannot be thwarted. None of Christ's true sheep will ever be lost. Though the elect may for a time fall into radical sin (such as Peter's denial of Christ), God restores them to fellowship with Himself and assures their eternal salvation. This salvation involves the work of the Trinity: All who are chosen by God the Father, redeemed by Christ the Son, and given faith by the Holy Spirit, are eternally saved. They are kept in faith by the power of Almighty God and thus persevere to the end. They persevere in faith because He preserves them. (John 3:16; 6:35-40; 6:44; 10:27-29; Rom. 8:28-39; Phil. 1:6; 2:12-13; Eph. 1:13-14; Jude 24-25)

I look back and see the whole thing—the desire to study these things and examine firmly held beliefs (I have found many do not wish to do this), and the ability to see the truth—as a work of God's grace in my life. How gracious it is that God opened up my eyes to see these things.

This book is not meant to be a treatise on these doctrines. There are very excellent works already in print that more than adequately discuss them (see the Recommended Reading section at the end of the book). My purpose in writing this book is much more streamlined and focused. I seek to provide answers to common objections that are often raised to the concept of Divine election and predestination.

I know these objections fairly intimately. In the past, I have raised every one of them. I am very much aware of the internal struggle that takes place when long held traditions are exposed to the light of Scripture and found wanting. It can be something of a revolution in the mind to understand just how Sovereign God is, and all the necessary consequences that this entails with such a big adjustment in thinking.

With that said, let me state what it is I am seeking to defend here. It is simply this:

God, before time began, chose a group of people out from the vastness of humanity who would be recipients of His mercy— "a great multitude that no one could number, from every nation, from all tribes and peoples and languages," (Rev. 7:9) who are called "the elect," or simply those "chosen by God."

Many Scriptures spell this out for us. Here are just a few of them:

"Blessed be the God and Father of our Lord Jesus Christ, who has blessed us in Christ with every spiritual blessing in the heavenly places, even as he chose us in him before the foundation of the world..." (Eph 1:3, 4)

"But for the sake of the elect, whom he chose, he shortened the days." (Mark 13:20)

"And he will send out his angels with a loud trumpet call, and they will gather his elect from the four winds, from one end of heaven to the other..." (Matt. 24:31)

"Who shall bring any charge against God's elect? It is God who justifies." (Rom. 8:33)

"But God chose what is foolish in the world to shame the wise; God chose what is weak in the world to shame the strong; God chose what is low and despised in the world, even things that are not, to bring to nothing things that are, so that no human being might boast in the presence of God." (1 Cor. 1:27-29)

"... as God's chosen ones, holy and beloved..." (Col. 3:12)

"But you are a chosen race, a royal priesthood, a holy nation, a people for his own possession, that you may proclaim the excellencies of him who called you out of darkness into his marvelous light..." (1 Pet. 2:9)

"God, who saved us and called us to a holy calling, not because of our works but because of his own purpose and grace, which he gave us in Christ Jesus before the ages began..." (2 Tim. 1:9)

"But we ought always to give thanks to God for you, brothers beloved by the Lord, because God chose you as the first-fruits to be saved, through sanctification by the Spirit and belief in the truth." (2 Thess. 2:13).

Some years back I was listening to a sermon by Dr. John MacArthur as he was discussing a passage in John chapter 6. I remember hurriedly writing down some notes as I was following along. I recently came across these notes and although this is not an actual transcript of what was said, I believe I was able to capture the main ideas. My notes read:

In the feeble understanding that our finite minds can grasp (we're on sacred ground here) there was a moment in eternity when the Father determined to express His infinite and perfect love for the Son (this love between the Persons of the Godhead is incomprehensible and inscrutable to us, it is so vast). But this we know about love: it gives. So at some eternal moment, the Father desired to express His perfect love for the Son. The way He determined to express that was to give to the Son a redeemed humanity as a love gift. The purpose of this redeemed humanity was to praise and glorify the Son throughout eternity and to serve Him perfectly. That was the Father's love gift. Evidently the planets wouldn't suffice. The angels wouldn't be enough either.

Not only did He decide to do this, but He decided who would make up this redeemed community and He wrote their names down in the Book of Life before the world began.

It was as if the Father said, "This is the love gift I want to give to You, and they will, forever and ever, praise and glorify Your name." The redeemed community in heaven is forever singing, "Worthy is the Lamb." In a certain sense, you and I are somewhat incidental here. Salvation is primarily for the honor of the Son, not the honor of the sinner. The purpose is not just so that the saved can enjoy a happy life knowing their sins are forgiven and heaven awaits them. That's a by-product. The purpose is to save you so that you could praise the Son for eternity.

John 6:37-44 "All that the Father gives me will come to me, and whoever comes to me I will never cast out. For I have come down from heaven, not to do my own will but the will of him who sent me. And this is the will of him who sent me, that I should lose nothing of all that he has given me, but raise it up on the last day. For this is the will of my Father, that everyone who looks on the Son and believes in him should have eternal life, and I will raise him up on the last day."

So the Jews grumbled about him, because he said, "I am the bread that came down from heaven." They said, "Is not this Jesus, the son of Joseph, whose father and mother we know? How does he now say, 'I have come down from heaven'?"

Jesus answered them, "Do not grumble among yourselves. No one can come to me unless the Father who sent me draws him. And I will raise him up on the last day."

Verse 37 states, "All that the Father gives me will come to me." Jesus is entrusted with a group known as the elect or the ones given to Him by His Father. These are a gift from the Father to the Son. Those given to the Son by the Father will come to Christ. It is inevitable that they will. And none in this group will ever be lost. They are secure because Jesus will finish the work His Father has given Him to do. None of the ones the Father chose to be His from eternity will be lost.

See the biblical sequence then found in verses 37-44 as outlined by MacArthur:

1. *All that the Father gives are drawn*

2. *All who are drawn come to Christ*

3. *All who come to Christ, Jesus receives (and He will never turn one of them away)*

4. *All who are drawn are raised up to eternal life*

This is not because the elect are inherently desirable!! It is because they are a gift from the Father to the Son. It is the perfect gratitude and love of the Son towards His Father that opens the arms of the Son to embrace the gift. Then verse 39 tells us that none of these will be lost.

The Father chooses these people; then writes their names down in the Lamb's book of life, which is a record of who that redeemed humanity will be. All in this group are then given to the Son as an expression of love.

Then in time, the Father draws all those within this group. When the Father draws them, these sinners come—all the Father gives to the Son will come to the Son. When these sinners come, the Son receives them. When the Son receives them, He keeps them and raises them on the last day, bringing the plan to fruition.

Verse 38 shows that He (Jesus) must do this—He comes down to do the Father's will. Jesus will not fail in this mission—He does the Father's will without fail.

What is the will of the Father that He is speaking of here?

Verse 39 "And this is the will of him who sent me, that I should lose nothing of all that he has given me, but raise it up on the last day."

Jesus said to them, "My food is to do the will of him who sent me and to accomplish his work." (John 4:34).

EAVESDROPPING ON A HOLY CONVERSATION

Obviously, we are on very sacred ground when we ponder such things, but here is a transcript from a C. H. Spurgeon sermon where he describes the eternal covenant of redemption and then wonders what it would have been like to have heard this covenant being made.

Now, in this covenant of grace, we must first of all observe the high contracting parties between whom it was made. The covenant of grace was made before the foundation of the world between God the Father, and God the Son; or to put it in a yet more scriptural light, it was made mutually between the three divine Persons of the adorable Trinity.

I cannot tell you it in the glorious celestial tongue in which it was written: I am fain to bring it down to the speech which suiteth to the ear of flesh, and to the heart of the mortal. Thus, I say, run the covenant, in ones like these:

I, the Most High Jehovah, do hereby give unto My only begotten and well-beloved Son, a people, countless beyond the number of stars, who shall be by Him washed from sin, by Him preserved, and kept, and led, and by Him, at last, presented before My throne, without spot, or wrinkle, or any such thing. I covenant by oath, and swear by Myself, because I can swear by no greater, that these whom I now give to Christ shall be forever the objects of My eternal love. Them I will forgive through the merit of the blood. To these will I give a perfect righteousness; these will I adopt and make My sons and daughters, and these shall reign with Me through Christ eternally.

Thus run that glorious side of the covenant. The Holy Spirit also, as one of the high contracting parties on this side of the covenant, gave His declaration, "I hereby covenant," saith He, "that all whom the Father giveth to the Son, I will in due time quicken. I will show them their need of redemption; I will cut off from them all groundless hope, and destroy their refuges of lies. I will bring them to the blood of sprinkling; I will give them faith whereby this blood shall be applied to them, I will work in them every grace; I will keep their faith alive; I will cleanse them and drive out all depravity from them, and they shall be presented at last spotless and faultless.

This was the one side of the covenant, which is at this very day being fulfilled and scrupulously kept. As for the other side of the covenant this was the part of it, engaged and covenanted by Christ. He thus declared, and covenanted with his Father:

My Father, on my part I covenant that in the fullness of time I will become man. I will take upon myself the form and nature of the fallen race. I will live in their wretched world, and for My people I will keep the law perfectly. I will work out a spotless righteousness, which shall be acceptable to the demands of Thy just and holy law. In due time I will bear the sins of all My people. Thou shalt exact their debts on Me; the chastisement of their peace I will endure, and by My stripes they shall be healed. My Father, I covenant and promise that I will be obedient unto death, even the death of the cross. I will magnify Thy law, and make it honourable. I will suffer all they ought to have suffered. I will endure the curse of Thy law, and all the vials of Thy wrath shall be emptied and spent upon My head. I will then rise again; I will ascend into heaven; I will intercede for them at Thy right hand; and I will make Myself responsible for every one of them, that not one of those whom thou hast given me shall ever be lost, but I will bring all my sheep of whom, by My blood, thou hast constituted Me the Shepherd — I will bring every one safe to Thee at last. (Sermon, The Blood of the Everlasting Covenant, delivered September 4th, 1859 at the Music Hall, Royal Surrey Gardens).

In "Mission Save the Elect" Jesus loses none of those given to Him in eternity past. As the angel said to Joseph, "You shall call his name Jesus, for he will save his people from their sins." (Matt. 1:21).It is true to say "Mission Save the Elect" becomes "Mission Accomplished." (Rev. 5:9).

WHAT IS "THAT"?

In my further studies into these matters, I found myself probing more deeply into very familiar passages of Scripture. One such passage was Ephesians 2:8, 9. In the NASB, it reads, "For by grace you have been saved through faith; and that not of yourselves, it is the gift of God; not as a result of works, so that no one may boast."

In these words, the Apostle Paul destroys all notions of salvation by works. We are saved by the grace of God, which is received through faith, and works play no part at all. As verse 10 makes clear, God has indeed planned for believers to do good works. But as this and many other passages in Scripture would affirm, the works are the fruit and not the root of our salvation. True believers do good works, but works play no role at all in how we receive salvation, for it is "not as a result of works."

This much is clear. But questions have arisen as to what exactly is meant by the one word "that" in Ephesians 2:8. We know that whatever it is, it is the gift of God, but can we determine exactly what this gift is?

Some say that the gift is "faith" while others say it is "grace" and still others say it is "salvation." What may be a point of dispute from the reading of the English translations becomes settled when looking into the original Greek text.

Putting it in terms we can hopefully all understand, the Greek word for "that" is transliterated into English as *touto* and is in a neuter form. The way to determine what it refers to is to look for the other neuter in the immediate context. That's how the issue would normally be resolved. Except that in this particular case, there isn't one. "Grace" is feminine; "have been saved" is masculine, and "faith" is also in a feminine form. In this case then, what the "that" refers to is all in the preceding clause. The grace, the salvation and the faith—all of these things—are the gift of God.

Paul is making it clear that nothing in our salvation comes from ourselves. Salvation, grace and faith—from start to finish, all of this is the gift of God, not as a result of works. God has designed salvation in this way for the very purpose of eliminating all grounds for human boasting. Boasting is not merely discouraged, or kept to a minimum, it is completely removed. That is because the entire work of salvation is God's work from start to finish—"this is not your own doing, it is the gift of God" as the ESV renders it. The grace by which we are saved and the faith that is the mechanism through which we receive it—yes, even this faith—are the gift of God. Salvation is of the Lord and all the glory for it goes to God alone.

Before we move on, I would like to quote one more verse. Actually, it is a phrase found in Acts 13 that is loaded with profound insight for us. In context, the apostles had preached the word of God, and simply as a commentary on the event, Luke (the writer) tells us the result he observed:

"…and as many as were appointed to eternal life believed.." (Acts 13:48).

It would be easy to just read this last text and hurriedly move on. Indeed, Luke does not stop to explain this statement. It seems to be just a casual observation on his part. Now he is ready to go on to the next thing. Pen (or more likely quill) in hand, Luke is ready to record for us the next event in the history of the ancient church.

But wait! Before we rush on to see the next thing that transpires in this exciting drama, let us just stop for a moment to think through the implications of Luke's statement. Luke wrote it, but it was the Holy Spirit who inspired it and no word here is wasted or superfluous. God intends us to see this event through the lens of His own perspective. He wants us to see something very powerful here.

What do I mean?

Well as we pause to consider the phrase, let us ask ourselves three questions:

"...and as many as were appointed to eternal life believed."

1. WHICH comes first—believing or being appointed to eternal life?

There is no getting around it, first there is the appointment to eternal life, and then there is the belief. There is a cause and effect relationship. The cause is the secret and unseen heavenly, eternal decree of God—the setting of an appointment; the effect is what is observed on the earth—the people responding in faith to the gospel. The cause is the appointment by God; the effect is the exercise of faith by man.

2. Do any MORE believe?

"... and as many as were appointed to eternal life believed."

The answer has to be "No." The number of people who believe are NO MORE than the many who were appointed to do so.

3. Do any LESS believe?

"...and as many as were appointed to eternal life believed."

Once again, the answer has to be "No."

ALL who had the appointment, made the appointment.

These are some very bold assertions, I am sure you will agree. Yet this is what Scripture teaches.

My own experience in seeing these Scriptures (and others) set before me, was to say to myself something like, "Sure, these are Scriptures which show God has an elect people whom He chooses unconditionally for salvation. But what about other Scriptures that would seemingly negate this idea?"

I am convinced that although the truths of God are often very mysterious, they are never contradictory. Therefore if, or rather since, God has made His word clear to us in the Scriptures quoted above, it is important to work through objections our traditional thinking often raises. And this is what we will seek to do in the rest of this work.

CHAPTER 4

WHAT ABOUT THE LOVE OF GOD? (Part 1)

One of the main reasons why some Christians reject the Reformed (and I believe biblical) understanding of Divine election is because of traditions associated with the love of God. The strong reaction of some against the doctrine of God's Sovereignty in election is often times due to a desire to defend what they believe to be the entire message of the Bible. They feel that God's attribute of love is in question or under attack. It is easy to see why this can become a very emotional issue for them.

Great care is needed to point people to the biblical texts that can clarify what is being said. Not everyone seems to be open to examining their assumptions because these traditions are so very strong. The tradition that God loves all people in exactly the same way is a strong one. I have to say, for many years, this was exactly the case in my own life.

Many see no need to examine the texts at all because in their minds, the concept they have of the love of God = what the Bible teaches. Dr. James White has rightly said, *The people who are most enslaved to their traditions are those who do not believe they have any.*

To gain a truly biblical understanding it is vital to recognize our assumptions and perceptions and then allow them to be held up to the light of Scripture to see if the Bible confirms them to be true. We are all prone to read into Scripture things that are not explicitly said and come away with traditions that are actually not taught by the Bible. That is why a prayerful and open heart and mind is so essential if we are going to allow Scripture to rule our thinking.

THE GREATEST NEED

What is the Church's biggest need? I believe that what the Church needs more than anything else is GOD as He really is, and the GOSPEL as it really is. If one of these is distorted, then so is the other.

If you are a genuine Christian, you have a desire to know the One true God as He has revealed Himself. You want to know Him and want to distance yourself from all concepts of Him that are not biblical. That's my assumption about you, the reader, as we explore this first chapter on the love of God.

Love is one of the attributes of God. The Bible tells us on almost every page of the wonderful love of God. "God is love." (1 John 4:8) What could be plainer than that?

Well actually, when we come to study the Bible, the doctrine of the love of God is far more complex than we may at first appreciate.

The task of the theologian is to take all the things the Bible tells us about a certain subject and make sense of it all. It is a science. Theology was once called the "Queen of the Sciences" as a person was said to have not gained a full education without completing a course in it. Theology simply means "the study of God" and everyone is a theologian in the sense that all people have some concept of God. Even atheists believe something about God; they deny His existence. So the question is not whether or not we will be theologians. That's a given. The question is: Are we going to be good ones or bad ones?

So where do we start when it comes to the love of God? We start by seeing where the love of God fits into the grand scheme of things. Here's what we know: God is. He is altogether perfect and does not need to change, for to admit the need to change would be an admission that what once was, was not entirely perfect. God is perfect in His attributes and has been forever. He always acts in conformity with who He is and therefore all He does is perfect. In Deuteronomy 32:3, 4, Moses wrote, "For I will proclaim the name of the LORD; ascribe greatness to our God! The Rock, his work is perfect, for all his ways are justice. A God of faithfulness and without iniquity, just and upright is he."

God has not changed in any way at all. Not recently. Not ever! God Himself says, "I am the Lord, I do not change." (Mal. 3:6).Yet in much of the church in our day, many of God's characteristics or attributes have been deliberately obscured from view. Oh, the more popular attributes of God are still being displayed, such as His love, His grace and His mercy. Yet there has been the obscuring of certain other attributes of God; namely His holiness, righteousness, justice, wrath and sovereignty. This indeed is a problem—a big problem.

Here's what I mean. At a buffet, we find no Buffet Police watching to see if we put every item on our plate, and holding us accountable for doing so. We are free to choose what type of food we will eat and what we will leave to one side. We do so with impunity, for we face no legal action for passing by a certain meat or failing to put the apple pie on our plate.

But let us be clear, God's attributes are not a buffet line of options. We are not invited to choose the attributes of God that we like best and leave the others. We have no right to say, "I'll give Sovereignty a pass, but I'll take the love." God doesn't allow us to put some of His attributes to one side. God is everything He says He is. To only believe in or to only emphasize certain of His characteristics is to invent our own god. There is a biblical name for that—idolatry! An idol can be fashioned and formed by the heart and mind just as much as by the hand. There is only one God and any god that is not the God who has revealed Himself in Scripture is a false one.

Romans 5:8-9 declares, "But God demonstrates His own love toward us, in that while we were yet sinners, Christ died for us. Much more then, having now been justified by His blood, we shall be saved from the wrath of God through Him."

Every sin man commits is an act of cosmic treason and as a Holy and just God, He is not only within His rights to be angry against us, He *must* be. For to treat sin lightly would mean that He was dismissive of His own holiness. Such a thing is impossible. Sin must be punished or else God is not just. If God is not just then God is not good. God is right to be full of wrath against His creatures. Yet, wrath is not the only attribute God displays. He displays great mercy. In fact, God in His love sent His Son into the world to save people from His own fierce wrath which is against all that have sinned against Him.

Romans 11:22 (KJV) says, "Behold the goodness and severity of God..." If we focus on only one of these attributes to the exclusion of the other, we distort the biblical picture of God. We also distort the gospel.

Hebrews 10:31 says, "It is a terrifying thing to fall into the hands of the living God." The ultimate calamity is to fall into the hands of the living God while not being in right standing with Him, facing the full judgment and wrath of God for eternity. If this is the greatest peril, then being rescued from this is the greatest deliverance and salvation.

At the cross, Jesus took all the sins of all those who would ever believe in Him and absorbed the full punishment of the Father's wrath against sin. He was the perfect, sinless Substitute who bore God's holy and just wrath, providing atonement and full propitiation (a propitiation is a sacrifice that removes wrath) for God's people. Wrath is only removed for believers. For the unbelievers, they stand under God's wrath. John 3:36 tells us, "Whoever believes in the Son has eternal life; whoever does not obey the Son shall not see life, but the wrath of God remains on him." If they remain defiant of God they will face the wrath of God in its fullness. Jesus' return to Earth will be marked by great joy and great fear. For although He is a shield to all who trust in Him, His wrath will be poured out on all those who are not His subjects.

Revelation 19:11-16 describes His fearful coming, "Then I saw heaven opened, and behold, a white horse! The one sitting on it is called Faithful and True, and in righteousness he judges and makes war. His eyes are like a flame of fire, and on his head are many diadems, and he has a name written that no one knows but himself. He is clothed in a robe dipped in blood, and the name by which he is called is The Word of God. And the armies of heaven, arrayed in fine linen, white and pure, were following him on white horses. From his mouth comes a sharp sword with which to strike down the nations, and he will rule them with a rod of iron. He will tread the winepress of the fury of the wrath of God the Almighty. On his robe and on his thigh he has a name written, King of kings and Lord of lords."

That's not the usual picture the Church portrays of Christ, but it is the biblical one. Unbelievers do not lie awake at night fearful of meeting God because all the Church has told them is "God loves you and has a wonderful plan for your life." They have no concept of the need to flee from the wrath to come. They feel no urgency. They've been told that God loves them unconditionally, which to them means that God is very happy with the way they've turned out. Certainly they do not feel the threat of Divine judgment. Why would they?

Yet the message of the Gospel is this: All who place their trust in Christ as Savior and Lord are therefore saved by God, from God, for God.

PENDULUM SWING

Though at one stage in Church history, the Church over-emphasized the wrath and judgment of God (many were rightly categorized as "hellfire and damnation preachers"); yet now the pendulum has fully swung the other way and all that many people have ever heard about is a very shallow and unbiblical presentation of the love of God.

I remember some time ago reading through the book of Acts taking special notice of the preaching of the Apostles. What was it that they preached? What did they emphasize? What was the sum and substance of the Apostle's preaching?

I was more than shocked when this process revealed that.. now wait for it.. the Apostles never mentioned the love of God.. not even once.

This is not to say that God doesn't love people. Far from it. But it was quite a shock to my thinking to realize that the love of God was not in view, especially as it is often the "only" thing in view in much of the Church world today.

In the New Testament there is a great deal said about the love of God, but the majority of it is written in the Epistles and is addressed to the Church.

In the next chapter I would like us to look at the multi faceted nature of God's love.

CHAPTER 5

WHAT ABOUT THE LOVE OF GOD? (Part 2)

As human beings, we are capable of both having and displaying different kinds of love. We love our favorite chair and we love our family, but hopefully not in the same way. If there was a fire in our home, the first thought would be to make sure all the family members were safely out of harm's way—the chair would be only an afterthought. We love our pets but we love our spouse more. We love our country far more than we love the electricity company that supplies power to our home.

Likewise God also has more than one degree or measure of love. His love is multi-faceted and multi-dimensional.

God the Father loves His eternal Son more than He loves the pigeon on my roof. He is loving to all His creatures and yet He is clear that He has a special love for His own elect people.

Certain people recoil from the ramifications of this saying, "But John 3:16 says that God so loved the WORLD that He gave His one and only Son..."

I have seen Christians play dueling verses as one quotes one Scripture while another quotes one that seemingly negates the first one. Such is only a display of immaturity. One says "God loves the world" as the other quotes Psalm 5:5, which tell us that God hates all evil doers.

Though John 3:16 rather than Psalm 5:5 is far more likely to be a verse displayed on our refrigerators, both are a part of the Scripture and the good theologian does not choose to believe one verse he likes more than the other but seeks to harmonize ALL that Scripture reveals.

I believe the answer to these kinds of potential dilemmas is to understand that God's love is multi-dimensional and multi-faceted. God has different degrees of love.

I will seek to deal with John 3:16 in a later chapter but for now, it is interesting to see that John uses the word "world" in at least ten different ways in his Gospel. World can mean:

1. The Entire Universe
John 1: 10 He was in the world (planet earth), and the world (planet earth and by implication all creation) was made through him, yet the world (the people of the world) did not know him.

John 17:5 And now, Father, glorify me in your own presence with the glory that I had with you before the world existed.

2. The Physical Earth
John 13:1 Now before the Feast of the Passover, when Jesus knew that his hour had come to depart out of this world to the Father, having loved his own who were in the world, he loved them to the end.

John 21:25 Now there are also many other things that Jesus did. Were every one of them to be written, I suppose that the world itself could not contain the books that would be written.

3. The World System
John 12:31 Now is the judgment of this world; now will the ruler of this world be cast out.

John 14:30 I will no longer talk much with you, for the ruler of this world is coming. He has no claim on me...

John 16:11 concerning judgment, because the ruler of this world is judged.

4. All humanity minus believers
John 7:7 The world cannot hate you, but it hates me because I testify about it that its works are evil.

John 15:18 If the world hates you, know that it has hated me before it hated you.

5. A Big Group but less than all people everywhere
John 12:19 So the Pharisees said to one another, "You see that you are gaining nothing. Look, the world has gone after him."

6. The Elect Only
John 3:17 For God did not send his Son into the world to condemn the world, but in order that the world might be saved through him.

7. The Non-Elect Only
John 17:9 I am praying for them. I am not praying for the world but for those whom you have given me, for they are yours.

8. The Realm of Mankind
John 1:10 He was in the world, and the world was made through him, yet the world did not know him.

(this is very probably the best understanding of the word "world" in John 3:16 also)

9. Jews and Gentiles (not just Israel but many Gentiles too)
John 4:42 They said to the woman, "It is no longer because of what you said that we believe, for we have heard for ourselves, and we know that this is indeed the Savior of the world."

10. The General Public (as distinguished from a private group)– –not those in small private groups
John 7:3, 4 So his brothers said to him, "Leave here and go to Judea, that your disciples also may see the works you are doing. For no one works in secret if he seeks to be known openly. If you do these things, show yourself to the world."

Seeing this list can be very helpful—especially when traditions reign supreme in some people's minds that "world" always means all people everywhere. Sometimes it does, but most of the time it does not. It is a tradition that is very strong but one that cannot survive biblical scrutiny.

Let us go further though and look at a passage of Scripture that gives us great insight as to the multi-dimensional character of God's love.

Romans 9:10-18

And not only so, but also when Rebekah had conceived children by one man, our forefather Isaac, though they were not yet born and had done nothing either good or bad—in order that God's purpose of election might continue, not because of works but because of him who calls— she was told, "The older will serve the younger." As it is written, "Jacob I loved, but Esau I hated."

What shall we say then? Is there injustice on God's part? By no means! For he says to Moses, "I will have mercy on whom I have mercy, and I will have compassion on whom I have compassion." So then it depends not on human will or exertion, but on God, who has mercy. For the Scripture says to Pharaoh, "For this very purpose I have raised you up, that I might show my power in you, and that my name might be proclaimed in all the earth." So then he has mercy on whomever he wills, and he hardens whomever he wills.

However we understand the phrase "Jacob I loved, but Esau I hated" in Romans 9, I think we would all have to agree that God's love for Jacob was certainly different or of a different kind than His love for Esau. This is the case or else the text is meaningless. But if this is so, then just this one verse refutes the idea that God loves everyone in the exact same way. There are different dimensions of the love of God.

Some seek to avoid this conclusion by saying that Jacob and Esau refer to nations rather than individuals. Certainly it is true that Jacob and Esau became mighty nations. However, the text itself refers to individual people (Jacob and Esau in the womb of their mother) and not nations, and even nations are made up of individuals. For God to set His love on a nation and reject another nation certainly has ramifications for the individuals within those nations—so the conclusion many are wanting to avoid (that God elects some but not all—and that He loves some in a special way that He does not love all) remains inescapable.

Let us remember the context here also. Paul is explaining why not all of the people of Israel have embraced their Messiah and come to salvation. He has just told us that God's word has not failed because not all Israel is Israel. (Rom. 9:6).Not all Israel in terms of physical descent is viewed as Israel in the eyes of God. All "Israel" (as God defined Israel) did embrace the Messiah (the Lord Jesus Christ) because they were the ones the promise was made to. That is the point of the passage and it is just this continued flow of thought from Romans 8 into Romans 9 that brings us to the "Jacob I loved, Esau I hated" statement.

The Apostle Paul is explaining why God's word does not fail in any way at all because all the Israel (as defined by God) will be saved and nothing can separate the true people of God from the love of God (something made clear in Romans 8). "Though they were not yet born and had done nothing either good or bad—in order that God's purpose of election might continue, not because of works but because of his call"—one brother was chosen and the other was not.

God has mercy on whom He will have mercy. God's electing purpose to set His electing love on Jacob and not on Esau is an EXPLANATION as to why God's word has not failed in any way at all. God's promise is true and His word always accomplishes its intended purpose. All the elect will receive this mercy. This is what the entire Romans 9 passage is teaching us. God's choice of one brother and not the other was not based on their actions (or works) but based on the powerful effectual call of God (something also made clear in Romans 8, where all the called are justified).

The fact is that God is Sovereign. As such, He reserves the right to have mercy on whom He will and to pass over others, leaving them in their hostile disposition against Him. God revealed Himself to Abraham in a way He did not for his neighbor down the street.

We read of God's mysterious love for Israel — mysterious because God never explains why He does so. He makes it clear that it was nothing in them that determined His choice. His love for them was far greater than other nations around them. He wanted a people for Himself and Sovereignly and unconditionally chose Israel to be His. In choosing Israel, He was not choosing the Hittites, the Amorites or the Philistines.

Here are God's own words to Israel, "For you are a people holy to the LORD your God. The LORD your God has chosen you to be a people for his treasured possession, out of all the peoples who are on the face of the earth. It was not because you were more in number than any other people that the LORD set his love on you and chose you, for you were the fewest of all peoples, but it is because the LORD loves you and is keeping the oath that he swore to your fathers, that the LORD has brought you out with a mighty hand and redeemed you from the house of slavery, from the hand of Pharaoh king of Egypt..." (Deut. 7:6-8)

After His resurrection, Christ appeared to Saul of Tarsus on the road to Damascus but not to Pontius Pilate in his bedroom. The whole Bible speaks of a God who is Sovereign in the way He bestows mercy.

And this is just it—many have come to me weeks after hearing me teach on this subject and, although they admitted to me that they were at first inwardly hostile and resistant to the teaching, after taking a second look and examining it for themselves (and as I say, not all are prepared to do this) they have made comments such as, "It is amazing! Now I see this truth everywhere I look in Scripture."

One person just recently told me, "I now see God's electing love in places I never imagined. I am reading my Bible and I am now seeing this in the parables of Jesus, and so many other places. I see that Jesus rejoiced that God's truth was hidden from some but revealed to others. I had read these kinds of passages for years and never seen it."

Luke 10:21 records Jesus rejoicing in the Holy Spirit and saying, "I thank you, Father, Lord of heaven and earth, that you have hidden these things from the wise and understanding and revealed them to little children; yes, Father, for such was your gracious will. All things have been handed over to me by my Father, and no one knows who the Son is except the Father, or who the Father is except the Son and anyone to whom the Son chooses to reveal him."

Commenting on these verses, another said, "It has rocked my world to understand that Jesus actually rejoiced that the Father hid truth from some. He rejoiced in His Father's electing love. What was once a loathsome thing, is sweetness and light, now I can see it."

If Jesus rejoices in His Father hiding (which speaks of activity) truth from some that He reveals to others, I think it should at least cause us to ask the question "why?"

Why would God hiding some things from some and revealing His truth to others be precious to our Lord? Why does it not excite us the way it excited Jesus? That is something to think about for sure.

As Romans 9 continues from verse 14, God sees it as perfectly just to dispense His mercy as He sees fit. Mercy, by its very definition, cannot be demanded. No one can demand mercy. The fact that no fallen angel will ever be redeemed causes no intellectual problem for the angels in heaven. God's just character remains intact and the angels of God continually sing, "Holy, holy, holy is the Lord of hosts."

What should surprise us about the text "Jacob I loved, but Esau I hated" is not that God hated Esau. Esau was a sinner and deserved the wrath of God just like the rest of us. What should astound us is that He set His love on Jacob. This should absolutely shock us! Why would God have anything to do with such a sinner? But sadly, we are not always astounded by this amazing mercy. I think that's because deep down, we tend to believe that everyone deserves mercy. The truth is that every one of us is every bit as much a sinner as Jacob. But until we as

Christians really "get" this, we do not grasp the amazing grace God has bestowed on us.

All people receive some mercy—God was very merciful to Esau, but ultimately Esau did not receive the exact same mercy as his brother Jacob. God sends His rain to all—on the just and the unjust. But He bestows His effectual, redeeming love only on some. Not everyone is saved. Some do perish. The fact that even one sinner will be numbered amongst the heavenly host because he was redeemed by the sheer mercy of God should amaze us. The fact is that this number will not be just a few, but will be so vast that no man can count it.

Revelation 7:9-10 After this I looked, and behold, a great multitude that no one could number, from every nation, from all tribes and peoples and languages, standing before the throne and before the Lamb, clothed in white robes, with palm branches in their hands, and crying out with a loud voice, "Salvation belongs to our God who sits on the throne, and to the Lamb!"

Hallelujah! What a Savior!

CHAPTER 6

WHAT ABOUT FREE WILL?

Why are you reading this? Yes, this particular sentence. There are billions of sentences out there just waiting to be read, in many different languages. But right now, you are reading this one. Why?

Well, it could be that some Reformed and crazed individual has put a gun to your head and told you that if you did not read these words he would shoot you. He would definitely be what some refer to as a caged stage reformer: after coming to understand the doctrines of grace, for a period of a couple of years or so, he needs to be locked up in a cage. His zeal for Reformation truth needs to be augmented with sanity in human relations! He sends books, tapes, CD's, mp3's, DVD's, and e-mails to all unsuspecting victims, regardless of whether or not they have ever shown an interest in these things. Christmas is his favorite time of the year, for he's been eagerly waiting for this opportunity to send R. C. Sproul's book *Chosen by God* to everyone he knows. He's on a mission alright, but the best thing would be for him to cool down for a couple of years in a cage!

However, even with the crazed reformed nut with a gun scenario, you are still making the choice to read these words rather than face the contents of the gun. You prefer to read this rather than to feel the impact of the bullet. Even now, you are reading this because you want to—right now you do, anyway. In fact, because this is your strongest inclination, there is no possible way for you to be reading anything else at this moment. It is impossible that you would be reading something other than this right now, and this will continue to be the case until you have a stronger desire to do or to read something else.

So what exactly is free will? Do people have it? Does God have it? How free is God's will? Can He do what He wants? Can we do what we want?

These kinds of questions are not new, of course. They have been the source of countless conversations and debates amongst ordinary folk and the chief theologians of the Church throughout history. Martin Luther, in looking back over his ministry considered his book on the subject of the will to be his most important work. In Luther's mind, to misunderstand the will is to misunderstand the Reformation doctrine of *sola gratia*. He stated, *If anyone ascribes salvation to the will, even in the least, he knows nothing of grace and has not understood Jesus Christ aright. (Luther, quoted by C.H. Spurgeon - New Park Street Pulpit, Sermon 52, Free will - a Slave, Vol. One, p. 395)*

I don't believe the issue is particularly complicated, which is why I am attempting to write a brief article on it here. This is not an entire treatise on the will. However, I think enough can be said in a short time to get all of us thinking.

Coming to an understanding of the human will, though not complicated, is often times hampered by our firmly-held traditions and man-centered tendencies. We are all born Pelagians at heart, thinking we can be anything we want to be, do anything we want to do, whether or not God has a will in the matter.

Human beings have wills. God has a will. But what exactly does this mean?

Can man do everything he chooses? Can man fly to the moon unaided by a machine? Can man go to the North Pole and survive with just a T-shirt, shorts and shoes on? Can man take a deep breath and live under water for a day without oxygen? No, man's free will is limited by his nature. It is not within man's nature and ability to fly to the moon unaided, to survive extreme cold without being sufficiently wrapped up, or to survive in water without oxygen. The problem is not the will—it is the nature of man. Because it is not man's nature to do a thing, he is not free to do the thing.

Have you noticed, though the term "free will" is bandied about every day, (other than in Old Testament passages speaking of "free will offerings" which simply refer to monetary gifts that are over and above what God demands in the law, and which are irrelevant to our discussion), you don't actually find the phrase in Scripture? That's because man's will has suffered a radical corruption in the Fall. Because our nature as unregenerate human beings has no interest in seeking after God (Romans 3:11), our will chooses, 100% of the time, to turn from God rather than towards him.

This is not due to some physical handicap, you understand, but rather a moral one—and one for which we are all responsible. Adam's sin brought the Fall, which had radical consequences for his progeny. As our federal head and perfect representative, Adam sinned on our behalf. But before we say it is not just for God to declare the entire human race guilty in Adam, we need to understand the other side of the coin. That is the wonderful truth that all who are in Christ are declared not guilty, and reckoned righteous with Christ's perfect righteousness. We can't believe in one of these imputations and not the other and still be biblical in our thinking.

We were all perfectly represented by Adam. He was a literal human personality, not a legend or myth. All of humanity were represented by Adam and reckoned guilty because of Adam's sin (Rom. 5:12, 19); all those in Christ (the Last Adam) are reckoned just because of Christ's righteousness (Rom. 5:17; 2 Cor. 5:21). As in Adam all die, so also in Christ shall all be made alive (1 Cor. 15:22).

Pastor Steve Weaver writes, *A good definition of free will is the ability of the mind to make choices in accordance with our natures. This definition of 'free will' also applies to God's free will. He too is bound by His nature. Therefore, He cannot sin! Why? Because it is not His nature! But God does have a free will and, unlike human beings, He has an accompanying good and holy nature.*

Jonathan Edwards said that the will is the mind choosing: though there is a distinction between mind and will, the two are inseparable in action. We do not make a choice without our mind's approval of that choice. We always act according to the strongest inclination at the moment of choice. We choose according to our strongest inclination at a given moment.

Why did you put on the particular clothes you are wearing today? It was because the things you put on had more of an appeal to you than anything else in your closet. Now, it may have been that there was nothing else available to you. Even so, your desire to wear something was greater than your desire to wear nothing, hence your choice. Again, we choose according to our strongest inclination at the moment of the choice.

When we commit a sin, at that moment our desire to sin is greater than our desire to obey Christ. I think that is the most haunting thing about the sins I commit. At that particular moment when I sinned, the sin was more appealing to me than obeying my Lord. This is the godly sorrow, I believe, that works repentance.

The Bible teaches that I am not free to choose God because it is contrary to my nature. That's why we need new natures that are given to us by the Holy Spirit at regeneration. Unless a man is born again, he cannot enter or even see the kingdom of God (John 3).

Though man is commanded to seek the Lord while He may be found and to come to Christ, we watch in vain for man to do so. Romans 3:11 literally reads, "There is no God seeker." John 6:44 says, "No one can come to me unless the Father who sent me draws him. And I will raise him up on the last day." Literally, the verse says, "no one is able."

Just like man is not able to fly to the moon unaided, the clear words of Christ here show that man is not able to come to Christ without Divine intervention. Here are some insights from Dr. R. C. Sproul concerning this verse:

First, we notice that Jesus said 'no one.' This is a universal negative statement. It does not mean that some cannot come unless the Father draws them. It means absolutely no one can come unless God does something first. Mankind is so depraved in fallen-ness that, apart from the irresistible grace of God, no one would ever turn to Christ.

Second, we notice that Jesus said 'can.' Remember the difference between the words can and may. Can means 'is able,' while may means 'has permission.' Jesus is not saying that no one has permission to come to him. Rather, he says that no one is able to come to him. This is the biblical doctrine of man's total inability.

Third, we notice the word 'unless.' This introduces an exception. Apart from this exception, no one would ever turn to Christ.

Finally we come to the word 'draw.' Some have said that draw only means 'woo' or 'entice.' That is not the case, however. In James 2:6 we read, 'Are they not the ones who are dragging you into court?' In Acts 16:19 we find, 'They dragged them into the marketplace.' The same Greek word is used in all three verses. Obviously, enticement is not in view here in John 6:44. Gerhard Kittel's Theological Dictionary of the New Testament says that the word translated draw in John 6:44 means 'to compel by irresistible authority.' It was used in classical Greek for drawing water from a well. We do not entice or persuade water to leave the well; we force it against gravity to come up by drawing it. So it is with us. We are so depraved that God must drag us to himself. (Chosen by God)

The wonder and beauty of God's grace is that while we are in a state of spiritual death, the Spirit's work is to make His elect willing to come. He changes the disposition of rebel human hearts, taking out a heart of stone, and putting in a heart of flesh so that they come willingly.

When most people quote John 6:44 they mention the first part of the verse: "No one can come to me unless the Father who sent me draws him," but they often fail to quote the rest of the verse, "And I will raise him up on the last day."

Jesus gives us very significant insight here and it is something we should not miss. He states that the one drawn is also raised up at the last day, signifying being raised to eternal life with Christ in heaven. The original words translated from *Koine* Greek into English are "... draws him and him I will raise up." The two "him's" are separated by only one Greek word.

This is important because linguistically there is no way to make the one drawn and the one raised up refer to two different people. The same one who is drawn is raised up to eternal life. Obviously, this is a powerful and effectual drawing resulting in salvation.

SOME FURTHER SCRIPTURES:

John 1:12-13 But to all who did receive him, who believed in his name, he gave the right to become children of God, who were born, not of blood nor of the will of the flesh nor of the will of man, but of God.

John 3:3 Jesus answered him, "Truly, truly, I say to you, unless one is born again he cannot see the kingdom of God."

John 6:36-37 But I said to you that you have seen me and yet do not believe. All that the Father gives me will come to me, and whoever comes to me I will never cast out.

John 8:33-34 They answered him, "We are offspring of Abraham and have never been enslaved to anyone. How is it that you say, 'You will become free'?"

Jesus answered them, "Truly, truly, I say to you, everyone who commits sin is a slave to sin."

John 8:47 Whoever is of God hears the words of God. The reason why you do not hear them is that you are not of God.

John 10:26-27 but you do not believe because you are not part of my flock. My sheep hear my voice, and I know them, and they follow me.

Romans 9:16 So then it (election) depends not on human will or exertion, but on God, who has mercy.

CHAPTER 7

WHAT ABOUT GOD'S FOREKNOWLEDGE?

Romans 8:28-30: And we know that for those who love God all things work together for good, for those who are called according to his purpose. For those whom he foreknew he also predestined to be conformed to the image of his Son, in order that he might be the firstborn among many brothers. And those whom he predestined he also called, and those whom he called he also justified, and those whom he justified he also glorified.

In what theologians refer to as "The Golden Chain of Redemption," God is revealing to us an unbreakable chain that starts in eternity past, goes through time, and on into eternity future. This chain is forged by God Himself, and has five unbreakable links: God foreknows, predestinates, calls, justifies and glorifies.

Notice that there is one ambiguity in the text; something that is not actually stated but is definitely implied—that being the word "all." Let's see this clearly by inserting another possible implication by way of contrast, the word "some."

"For (some) whom He foreknew, He predestined; (some) He predestined, He called; (some) He called, He justified; and (some) He justified, were glorified." What kind of comfort and security would that give to us? Would we be able to say "Who can separate us from the love of Christ?"

I think our answer would have to be that many things could separate us (if the intended implication was the word "some" in this passage). It would make absolutely no sense whatsoever and certainly would not give us any kind of security in Christ, the very thing Paul is seeking to do in this Romans 8 passage.

I believe 100 out of 100 Bible scholars would all agree that the implication of the text is that all He foreknew, He predestined; all He predestined, He called; all He called, He justified; and all He justified, He glorified.

FOR THOSE WHOM HE FOREKNEW...

In Romans 8:29, the text reads "For those whom he foreknew, he also predestined to become conformed to the image of His Son..."

Does this not therefore suggest that because foreknowledge comes before predestination in the text, then predestination is simply based on God's foreknowledge? In other words, because God foreknows or sees in advance (with full and complete knowledge) what a person will do, and who it is that will respond in faith to the Gospel, He simply predestinates those whom He knows will believe. Right?

Certainly this is how I understood this passage for many years and it is the way that many deal with the issue of predestination in our day.

I also pointed to 1 Peter 1:1-2 which talks of those who are "elect ... according to the foreknowledge of God the Father..." and assumed that this verse would add weight to my argument that election and predestination is based on God knowing ahead of time what we will do.

At first glance, it certainly seems to be a legitimate interpretation, because the word "foreknew" comes before "predestination" in the text of Romans 8:29.

However, the fact that foreknowledge comes before predestination should in no way surprise us. That's because God would need to foreknow a person He is going to predestinate to something. God does not predestinate unknown persons, but specific individuals whom He knows.

So this is not really an argument for either side in this debate. In both systems, foreknowing would need to come before predestination.

The real question then is, "What exactly does it mean for God to *foreknow* somebody?"

Actually there are a number of problems with the way I once understood "foreknowledge"—not the least of which is that Scripture reveals very clearly that, left to himself, man will always choose against Christ, because of his hostile disposition to God. Man is dead spiritually and needs his heart of stone to be removed and a heart of flesh put in before he has any interest in seeking the God of the Bible. (Rom. 3:11; Rom. 8:7, 8; 1 Cor. 2:14). Apart from regeneration, man is the sworn enemy of God.

As A. W. Pink once stated, *God did not elect any sinner because He foresaw that he would believe, for the simple but sufficient reason that no sinner ever believes until God gives him faith, just as no man sees until God gives him sight.* (Pink, *The Nature of God*)

The interpretation also falls down because the word "foreknew" does not merely mean to know future actions beforehand. It has a much more precise meaning. The word "foreknew" (Greek: *proginosko*) in Romans 8:29 is a verb rather than a noun. It is an action word. And as the text informs us, it is something done by God. What exactly does God do then? The text says that "those whom he foreknew..."

To gain a correct biblical definition of this word foreknew, rather than assume its meaning, (which is what many do) we need to do some homework and study. In this case it means we need to go to passages of Scripture that have God as the subject of the verbal form (as here in this passage). This is because passages that have humans as the subject would differ substantially in their meaning from the ones where God is the subject. I am sure we will all agree, we as creatures "know" things on a very different basis to the way God does.

When we do this we find the verb *proginosko* is used three times in the New Testament with God as the subject—here in Romans 8:29, then also in Romans 11:2, and lastly in 1 Peter 1:20.

This proves to be significant when we ask the question, "What, or who is foreknown by God?"

In Romans 8:29, the direct object of the verb is a pronoun that refers back to the called of the previous verse (v. 28). In Romans 11:2 the object the verb is referring to is "His people." And in 1 Peter 1:20, the object is Jesus Christ Himself.

Each reference then portrays God as foreknowing persons rather than actions. 1 Peter 1:20 says, "He was foreknown before the foundation of the world but was made manifest in the last times for the sake of you." When God foreknew Christ, did that mean that God simply knew that Jesus would make correct decisions or have faith in His Father? Hardly! It speaks of the Father's personal intimacy and affection for His beloved Son.

To say that God foreknows acts, faith, behavior, choices, etc, is to assume something about the term that is not witnessed in the biblical text. God "foreknows" persons not actions. Of course, God does know the future actions of people, but that is not how the word "foreknow" is used biblically—ever.

How does this relate to what we see in the Old Testament? Well there, we encounter a similar word use to "foreknew" in the New Testament, found in the Hebrew word "yada." It refers in a number of instances to God's "knowing" of individuals.

For instance in Jeremiah 1:5, God said to Jeremiah, "Before I formed you in the womb I knew you, and before you were born I consecrated you; I appointed you a prophet to the nations."

We see this same concept in God's "knowing" of Moses. Exodus 33:17—"And the LORD said to Moses, 'This very thing that you have spoken I will do, for you have found favor in my sight, and I know you by name.'" Again we see the personal nature of God's knowing of an individual. This refers to a personal intimacy and affection God had for Moses in that he had found favor in the eyes of the Lord. God had chosen Moses to be a recipient of His tender mercy.

I'll quote just one more passage where we see this word *yada* used to refer to God possessing a personal intimacy and affection. Amos 3:2 in speaking of Israel says, "You only have I known of all the families of the earth; therefore I will punish you for all your iniquities." Though the ESV translates the word *"yada"* here as "known," the NASB actually translates it as "chosen," and there is a very strong basis by way of context for this word to be translated in this way. Literally it says, "You (speaking of Israel) only have I known..."

It should be obvious to us that God did not merely know about Israel and possessed no such knowledge of other nations, nor that God merely knew the future actions of Israel and did not know the future actions of the other nations. This "knowing" of Israel is deeply personal and intimate. It speaks of God's grace in choosing them to be His people for His Sovereign purposes alone. The word *yada* is used also in Genesis 4:1 when it says that Adam "knew" his wife Eve. The result of this "knowing" was a child, revealing a deep personal relationship.

All this is important because it presents a consistent pattern. Understanding how the verb is used in the New Testament, along with these insights from the Old, provides a very strong basis for understanding what foreknew actually means.

Dr. White in his book *The Potter's Freedom* states, *When Paul says, 'those whom He foreknew' Paul is speaking about an action on God's part that is just as solitary, just as God-centered, and just as personal as every other action in the string: God foreknows (chooses to enter into relationship with); God predestines; God calls; God justifies; God glorifies. From first to last it is God who is active, God who accomplishes all these things.*

Foreknew therefore does not merely suggest "a passive gathering of infallible knowledge of the future actions of free creatures," but rather reveals that from start to finish, salvation is a Divine accomplishment. It is God and God alone who saves, to the praise of His glory alone.

To quote Dr. James Montgomery Boice in his comments on Romans 8:29, "those whom God foreknew: *The verse does not say that God foreknew what certain of his creatures would do.*

It is not talking about human actions at all. On the contrary, it is speaking entirely of God and of what God does. Each of these five terms is like that: God foreknew, God predestined, God called, God justified, God glorified. Besides, the object of the divine foreknowledge is not the actions of certain people but the people themselves. In this sense it can only mean that God has fixed a special attention upon them or loved them savingly.

ESTABLISHING THE MESSAGE OF GRACE

Romans 11:5,6 declares, "So too at the present time there is a remnant, chosen by grace. But if it is by grace, it is no longer on the basis of works; otherwise grace would no longer be grace."

Allow me to quote Mark Webb here:

The most casual Bible student admits that Scripture indeed employs the language of election when speaking of God's eternal purposes. Yet most seek to dodge the implications of that language by fleeing to the refuge of 'conditional' election (i.e. that God's choice, or election, of certain men to salvation is "conditioned" by his foreseeing faith in those men)...

If "conditional" election is true—if God's choice of me is determined by my choice of Him—the practical effect of this teaching is no different than if there were no election at all! The proof of this assertion is seen in the fact that the groups who hold this view seldom, if ever, mention the subject. And why should they? To what purpose? Since it's taught that God has done all He can do to save, and now it's up to man, the will of man becomes the determining and dominant factor in salvation. Whenever you make God's choice of men to salvation hinge upon what He foresees in man—be it his work, his faith, or his choice—you have effectively undermined the whole concept of salvation by grace alone! Either salvation depends upon God's free choice and good pleasure, which is the principle of "grace," or it depends upon something man himself produces, which is the principle of "works." It really matters not whether this "thing" which God foresees is something tangible, seen outwardly in the man's life, or something intangible, seen inwardly only by God. It matters not whether it's a huge thing, or whether it's a tiny thing. So long as man's part is the critical, determinative part, you have a system based upon "works" not grace.

Let me illustrate. Suppose you came to me and said, "Mark, I have a $15,000 car here. If you'll pay me $15,000, I'll give you the car." We'd all agree, that's not "grace," that's "works." But suppose you said, "Mark, I've a $15,000 car here, and I'll simply give you the car." We'd all agree, that's "grace," not "works."

But now let's try to mix the two concepts. Suppose you said, "Mark, here's a $15,000 car. I'll be $14,999 gracious to you if you'll simply pay me $1." Have we succeeded in mixing "grace" and "works?" No! For what's the practical difference between that last offer and you simply saying, "Mark, here's a $15,000 car—I'll sell it for $1?" Do you see? You're still coming to me on the basis of "selling," not "giving." You've not changed your principle, you've simply lowered your price!

This is precisely Paul's point in Romans 11:5-6. An "unconditional" election is the only concept of election consistent with salvation by free grace!... God intentionally designed salvation so that no man could boast of it. He didn't merely arrange it so that boasting would be discouraged or kept to a minimum—He planned it so that boasting would be absolutely excluded! Election does precisely that.—What Difference Does it Make? A Discussion of the Evangelical Utility of the Doctrines of Grace.

Before we move on, let us also look at this from a logical perspective of what God knew from eternity.

As John Hendryx has stated, *If God knew someone would choose hell even before He created them, then this was a fixed certainty (even before their creation), so why did God go ahead and create them? It was obviously, in their view, still within His Providence that these people be lost... or if God already foreknew who would be saved then how can they continue to argue that He is trying to save every man? Certainly God already knows who the persons will be, so why should He send the Holy Spirit to those He knows will reject him?* (monergism.com).Ultimately, when this view is subjected to scrutiny, it logically undermines the very position it is seeking to assert.

"But," say others, "God elected them on the foresight of their faith." Now, God gives faith, therefore he could not have elected them on account of faith, which he foresaw. There shall be twenty beggars in the street, and I determine to give one of them a shilling; but will anyone say that I determined to give that one a shilling, that I elected him to have the shilling, because I foresaw that he would have it? That would be talking nonsense. In like manner to say that God elected men because he foresaw they would have faith, which is salvation in the germ, would be too absurd for us to listen to for a moment. - C. H. Spurgeon, from the sermon "Election," preached on September 2, 1855, at New Park Street Chapel, Southwark.

CHAPTER 8

WHAT ABOUT JOHN 3:16?

The question usually posed here is something like this: How can you reconcile belief in Divine election with John 3:16?

Most assume it is not possible. Actually, if we carefully take a look at the text and not just assume its meaning, John 3:16 is a wonderful Scripture that in no way undermines the truth of Divine election.

It is certainly the most famous verse in the entire Bible. Here Jesus says: "For God so loved the world, that he gave his only Son, that whoever believes in him should not perish but have eternal life."

When hearing the biblical teaching on the subject of Divine election, some seek immediate refuge in a traditional, and may I say unbiblical, understanding of this verse.

They say this: "God can't elect certain ones to salvation because John 3:16 says that God so loved the world that gave His Son so that WHOEVER believes in Christ would have eternal life. Therefore, God has done His part in offering the gift of salvation in His Son and just leaves it up to us to receive the gift through faith. Amen. Case closed!"

Though this is a very common tradition, and one I held to myself for many a year, it needs to be pointed out that in spite of the emphasis made by many people on the word "whoever," the text does not actually discuss who does or does not have the ability to believe.

Someone might just as well be quoting John 3:16 to suggest that all churches need to have red carpets in their sanctuaries! Why? Because that also is not a topic addressed in the text. The verse is often quoted, but actually it has no relevance to the subject.

For the understanding of a text in the New Testament, we need to check the original language in which it was written, namely *Koine* Greek. It may come as a big surprise to learn that in the original Greek of John 3:16, there is no word corresponding to our English word "whoever." The word "whoever" is expressing a phrase in Greek which is difficult to express smoothly in English.

Literally, the text reads "in order that every the one believing in Him, not to perish, but have everlasting life."

It says "every" or "all the ones believing..." That's hard to express in English. But in essence, it is saying "all the believing ones." That's what is being communicated. It is saying that there is no such thing as a believing one who does not receive eternal life, but who perishes. Though our English translation says "whoever believes," the literal rendering is accurately translated as "every believing one" and the emphasis is NOT AT ALL on the "whosoever," but on the belief. The ones BELIEVING will not have one consequence, but will have another. They will not perish but will have everlasting life.

Why? Because of the main verb—God GAVE His Son. God gave His Son for the purpose (Greek: *hina*) that every believing one should not perish, but that every believing one should have everlasting life.

John 3:16 actually speaks of a limitation—of a particular, rather than a universal, redemption. For clearly, not everyone will be saved. Only those who believe in Christ are saved. The Father loved the world in this way: He gave His Son for the purpose of saving those who believe. The Son is given so that the believing ones will not perish, but by contrast, have eternal life. That is the purpose of the giving.

So, what John 3:16 teaches is:

ALL who do A (believe in Him)
will not B (perish)
but will have C (everlasting life)

What does this text tell us about who will believe or who can believe?

The answer is: ABSOLUTELY NOTHING! The text does not address the issue of who will believe or who can believe.

However, if you do want to know John's view on who can exercise faith, he does deal with that question—just not in this text. If you go back a few verses in the chapter to John 3:3, John quotes Jesus as saying "unless a man is born again he cannot enter the kingdom of God." That's clear, isn't it?

Jesus said that a prerequisite, a necessary condition that must be met before someone can enter the kingdom of God, is that they are born again. We enter the kingdom of God through faith. But in order to enter the kingdom, we must first be born again, or made spiritually alive. If we are not FIRST born again, we cannot enter the kingdom of God.

This same issue is certainly addressed by Jesus, 3 chapters further on, in John 6:44, when He said, "No one can come to me unless the Father who sent me draws him. And I will raise him up on the last day." It should be noted that the one drawn by the

Father to the Son is also raised up on the last day to eternal life. (John 6:39, 40).

In John 6:65, Jesus said, "This is why I told you that no one can come to me unless it is granted him by the Father."

Of course, all who exercise true faith will certainly be saved. John 3:16 clearly teaches that. Anyone believing in Christ will not perish but have everlasting life.

But what we need to ask is, "Who will have faith?"

The Reformed, and biblical, view is that only the elect will be brought to faith. No one can come to Christ unless God does something to enable that person to come.

So why do people miss what John 3:16 teaches or read into it (eisegesis) what is not actually in the text?

That's easy. It is because of how they have heard John 3:16 used over and over and over again. They have an ingrained, preconceived notion of what the verse says, and fail to question that assumption and read the text for what it actually says.

It's a tradition. And if you dare question it, you might be accused of questioning the very word of God, rather than their traditional interpretation of the word of God. And that can create a whole lot of emotion.

This text, of course, is just one example of many that could be quoted, but it does show us how powerful our traditions can be. We need to continuously expose our traditions to the light of God's Word. If they can be confirmed by detailed study of the text of Scripture, we can be sure that the traditions are valid. If not, then we need to dispense with them. Let God be true and every man a liar... even if the "man" here refers to our own firmly held beliefs, but not the testimony of Scripture itself.

CHAPTER 9

WHAT ABOUT 2 PETER 3:9?

Without doubt, this is the single most popular verse used to dismiss the biblical doctrine of election, bar none. The meaning of the verse is simply assumed, and because of this, no time is taken to study it, which is the very hallmark of tradition. I have to admit that I did this for many years. Those most enslaved to tradition are those who think they do not have any.

First of all then, let us read the verse in its context:
2 Peter 3:1-9—"This is now the second letter that I am writing to you, beloved. In both of them I am stirring up your sincere mind by way of reminder, that you should remember the predictions of the holy prophets and the commandment of the Lord and Savior through your apostles, knowing this first of all, that scoffers will come in the last days with scoffing, following their own sinful desires. They will say, 'Where is the promise of his coming? For ever since the fathers fell asleep, all things are continuing as they were from the beginning of creation.' For they deliberately overlook this fact, that the heavens existed long ago, and the earth was formed out of water and through water by the word of God, and that by means of these the world that then existed was deluged with water and perished. But by the same word the heavens and earth that now exist are stored up for fire, being kept until the day of judgment and destruction of the ungodly.

But do not overlook this one fact, beloved, that with the Lord one day is as a thousand years, and a thousand years as one day.

The Lord is not slow to fulfill his promise as some count slowness, but is patient toward you, not wishing that any should perish, but that all should reach repentance."

The first thing we notice is that the subject of the passage is not salvation but the second coming of Christ. Peter is explaining the reason for the delay in Christ's second coming. He is still coming and will come unexpectedly, like a thief in the night (v. 10).

The second thing to notice is that the verse in question (v. 9) speaks of the will of God. "God is not willing" for something to happen.

Theologians have long recognized that there are three ways in which the will of God is spoken of in Scripture.

There is what is called the **Sovereign Decretive Will.** This refers to the will by which God brings to pass whatsoever He decrees. This is something that ALWAYS happens. Nothing can thwart this will. (Isa. 46:10, 11).This will is also known as the secret will of God because it is hidden to us until it comes to pass in the course of time.

Secondly, there is the **Preceptive Will of God.** This is God's will revealed in His law, commandments or precepts. As the course of human history reveals, people have the power to break these commandments and do so every day. It is important to state though that, although men have the power to break these precepts, they do not have the right to do so. His creatures are under obligation to obey all His commandments and will face His judgment for not doing so.

Thirdly, we have God's **Will of Disposition.** Dr. R. C. Sproul states, *This will describes God's attitude. It defines what is pleasing to Him. For example, God takes no delight in the death of the wicked, yet He most surely wills or decrees the death of* *the wicked. God's ultimate delight is in His own holiness and righteousness. When He judges the world, He delights in the vindication of His own righteousness and justice, yet He is not gleeful in a vindictive sense toward those who receive His judgment. God is pleased when we find our pleasure in obedience. He is sorely displeased when we are disobedient. (Essential Truths of the Christian Faith)*

There are many in the Reformed community who look at 2 Peter 3:9 and feel that what we have here is God expressing His will of disposition. They believe the text to be saying that God is not wishing or desiring to see any human being perish (in one sense), even though that is exactly what will happen if a person does not come to repentance. The fact that people perish is not something that makes God happy. He would rather it never happened. But to uphold His holiness and justice, He must punish rebellious sinners by sending them to an eternity in hell.

A lot could be said for this view of the text and I have many Reformed friends who hold to it. It does seem to solve many problems. However, I take a different view because of what I see when I follow the pronouns of the passage.

WHO ARE THE "ALL"?

The people Peter is addressing are clearly identified. He speaks of the mockers as "they", but everywhere else he speaks to his audience as "you" and the "beloved." I believe this is very important.

But surely "all" means "all," right? Well usually, yes, but not always. This has to be determined by the context in which the words are found. When a school teacher is in a classroom and is about to start the class and asks the students, "Are we all here?" or "Is everyone here?" he is not asking if everyone on planet Earth is in the classroom. Because of the context in which the question is framed, we understand that he is referring to all within a certain class or type—in this case, all the students in the class. To say that he is referring to all people on planet earth would be to grossly misinterpret the intended meaning of his question.

So, the question in 2 Peter 3:9 is whether "all" refers to all human beings without exception, or whether it refers to everyone within a certain group.

The context of 2 Peter 3:9 indicates that Peter is writing to a specific group and not to all of mankind. The audience is confirmed when Peter writes, "This is now the second letter that I am writing to you, beloved..." (2 Peter 3:1).

Can we be even more specific? Yes, because if this is the second letter addressed to them, the first makes it clear who he is writing to. 1 Peter 1:1—"Peter, an apostle of Jesus Christ, To those who are elect..."

So Peter is writing to the elect in 2 Peter 3:8, 9 saying "But do not overlook this one fact, **beloved**, that with the Lord one day is as a thousand years, and a thousand years as one day. The Lord is not slow to fulfill his promise as some count slowness, but is patient toward **you**, not wishing that any should perish, but that all should reach repentance."

I would agree with Dr. Sproul (and other scholars) who believe that the will of God spoken of here is not God's will of disposition but His Sovereign decretive will. God is not willing that any should perish. He will not allow it to happen.

Allowing for this premise then, if the "any" or "all" here refers to everyone in human history, the verse would prove universalism rather than Christianity. (Universalism is the false doctrine that teaches that everyone will in the end be saved, with no one going to hell). If God is not willing (in His decretive Sovereign will) that any person perish; then what? No one would ever perish! Yet, in context, the "any" that God wills not to perish is limited to the same group he is writing to, the elect; and the "all" that are to come to repentance is the very same group.

This interpretation makes total sense of the passage. Christ's second coming has been delayed so that all the elect can be gathered in. The elect are not justified by election, but by putting their faith in Christ. If a person is to be saved they must come to Christ in repentance and faith. The doctrine of Sovereign Election simply explains who will do so. The elect will.

Jesus assured us of this when He said, "All that the Father gives to me will come to me" (John 6:37) and is confirmed by the testimony of Luke in Acts 13:48 when he observed that "... all who were appointed to eternal life believed."

2 Peter Chapter 3 teaches us that the reason Christ has not yet returned is because there are more of His elect to come into the fold. That is why He did not return yesterday. At this point in time, not all of the elect have come to repentance and faith. Therefore Christ has not yet returned to the Earth in power and glory. Christ's second coming may seem delayed (to some) but God is being very longsuffering toward us (you, beloved) not willing that any should perish but that all come to repentance. Speaking personally, I am so glad that the Lord Jesus did not return the day before I was converted. I would have been lost in sin forever.

Rather than denying election, the verse, understood in its biblical context, is one of the strongest verses in favor of it. The context of 2 Peter 3 shouts and screams that Peter, when writing of "all," is actually referring to all of the elect.

CHAPTER 10

WHAT ABOUT 1 TIMOTHY 2:4?

How can Sovereign election be true when 1 Timothy 2:4 clearly says that God "desires all people to be saved and to come to the knowledge of the truth"?

In the previous chapter, I mentioned that some biblical scholars whom I greatly respect interpret the 2 Peter 3:9 text through the lens of what they see as God's will of disposition. Many of these same scholars would interpret 1 Timothy 2:4 in a similar way. They would say that God desires that all people be saved and come to the knowledge of the truth (in one sense) but that He also allows for many people to resist this will and, in doing so, be lost forever. Once again, much could be said for this interpretation. Yet once again, I believe a close examination of the text itself points us in a different direction, which I will seek to outline here.

Before I do so, let me just say that it is entirely possible to go for many years without asking questions about a text of Scripture because we assume we have already understood it. This is the very hallmark of tradition. Blind to our own assumptions we see no need to look at the text objectively and see if our understanding of the text can be verified by the text itself. However, if we take a deep breath and summon up the courage to ask the simple question, "What does the context tell us about the use of the word "all" here in this text?" I believe we will come away with the correct interpretation. Actually, it is absolutely vital we do this because context tells us how a word is being used.

THE MEANING OF THE WORD "ALL"

The word translated "all" in 1 Timothy 2:4 is the Greek word "pas." As I also mentioned in the last chapter, sometimes the word "all" refers to all people everywhere. On other occasions it means "all kinds" or "all classes or types" or "all within a certain type or class."

In the same letter, written obviously by the same author, Paul, we read the very familiar words of chapter 6 and verse 10, "For the love of money is the root of all evil..." (KJV).

More modern scholarship recognizes that the word "pas" sometimes means "all" and sometimes means "all types" or "all kinds," depending on the context in which it is found. Therefore the ESV translation of 1 Timothy 6:10 is "For the love of money is a root of all kinds of evils." The NASB says, "For the love of money is a root of all sorts of evil..." The NIV reads, "For the love of money is a root of all kinds of evil." Again, the Greek word "pas" can mean "all types" or "all kinds."

I mention this because when we examine 1 Timothy 2:4, I believe the word "all" is being used in a similar sort of way, referring to "all types" of people. I say this based on the context.

Here is the passage in 1 Timothy 2:1-4:

"First of all, then, I urge that supplications, prayers, intercessions, and thanksgivings be made for all people, for kings and all who are in high positions, that we may lead a peaceful and quiet life, godly and dignified in every way. This is good, and it is pleasing in the sight of God our Savior, who desires all people to be saved and to come to the knowledge of the truth."

Who are the "all people" of verse 1?

This is a very important question because I believe the "all people" of verse 1 are the same "all people" of verse 4, as the subject matter does not change in any way at all in the intervening verses.

When Paul wrote "First of all, then, I urge that supplications, prayers, intercessions, and thanksgivings be made for all people," was he asking Timothy to get the equivalent of the local phone book and starting with the alphas and going all the way through to the omegas (the Greek alphabet), begin to make supplication, pray, intercede and give thanks for each individual in the city... or more than that, the whole world? I don't think so. Why do I say this?

Because Paul qualifies verse 1 with verse 2 when he speaks of "kings" (kings are types of people) and "those in high positions" (note again "those in high positions" are types of people).

Why should we pray for them?

One of the reasons we should pray for them is because these people (kings and those in high positions of authority) make decisions which affect society at large. If these people have their eyes opened, they will not be persecutors of Christians but will enact laws that will actually restrain sin so "that we may lead a peaceful and quiet life, godly and dignified in every way." We are to pray for these leaders because good government can mean a measure of peace in a society. And it is a lot easier to spread the Gospel when there is no civil unrest.

The passage also points us to another reason to pray, namely that God desires all (all who?)—all types of people, including these influential people with authority in society—to be saved.

His message to Timothy was this: Do not just pray for the peasants, the farmers and the uneducated (the people who seem to be coming to Christ in great numbers at the moment), but remember to pray for kings and the very rulers in society who are persecuting Christians. Make prayer of this kind a priority. Do it "first of all." Pray for these people Timothy. Make sure the Church is praying for these people, because God desires all kinds of people—even kings (or Emperors like Caesar) and the elite in society—people of every kind, to be saved.

We must remember that the earliest Christians were almost all from the lower class of society, so this would be BIG news to them. As Paul wrote elsewhere in 1 Corinthians 1:26-29 26, "For consider your calling, brothers: not many of you were wise according to worldly standards, not many were powerful, not many were of noble birth. But God chose what is foolish in the world to shame the wise; God chose what is weak in the world to shame the strong; God chose what is low and despised in the world, even things that are not, to bring to nothing things that are, so that no human being might boast in the presence of God."

Let us now go back to the passage in 1 Timothy 2, for there is still much more to glean. Normally the verses that follow on from v. 4 are not brought into the equation, but they should be. The very next word (after verse 4) is the word "for," which is a linking word, connecting what has been said with that which is to follow.

Why are we to pray for all kinds of men to be saved and come to the knowledge of the truth?

The answer is "For there is one God, and there is one mediator between God and men, the man Christ Jesus, who gave himself as a ransom for all, which is the testimony given at the proper time." (v. 5, 6)

IF all men refer to all individuals on planet Earth we are faced with two huge theological issues. Dr. James White outlines the problems this way:

First, if one takes "all men" in verse 4 to mean "all men individually," does it not follow that Christ of necessity must be mediator for all men as well? If one says, "Yes, Christ mediates for every single human being," does it not follow that Christ fails as mediator every time a person negates His work by their all-powerful act of free will? One could hope that no biblical scholar would ever promote such an idea, for anyone familiar with the relationship between atonement, mediator and intercession in the book of Hebrews knows well that to make such an assertion puts the entire argument of Hebrews 7-10 on its head. For the moment, we simply point out that it is far more consistent with biblical theology to recognize that Christ mediates in behalf of the elect and perfectly saves them than it is to assert that Christ mediates for all (but fails to save all).

The second point is closely related to the first: the ransom that Christ gives in His self-sacrifice is either a saving ransom or a non-saving one. If it is actual and really made in behalf of all men, then inevitably all men would be saved. But we again see that it is far more consistent to recognize that the same meaning for "all men" and "all" flows through the entire passage, and when we look at the inarguably clear statements of Scripture regarding the actual intention and result of Christ's cross-work, we will see there is no other consistent means of interpreting these words in 1 Timothy. (The Potter's Freedom, p. 142)

We must understand that the function or purpose of a mediator is to mediate—to come between two estranged parties in order to bring them together. Now, if "all men" refers to every individual on earth, then firstly, Christ often fails in his work as the mediator—for the Scripture makes it plain that God's wrath will indeed be poured out on many in hell. Secondly, we are left with a ransom that, in the case of those who do end up in hell, does not actually pay for sin—they are in hell paying for their sin. If Christ actually paid for the sins of those who end up in hell, what did Christ's sacrifice actually achieve for them? The answer is: nothing at all. We would be left with an atonement that does not actually atone—a mere hypothetical redemption that achieves nothing in all actuality for the lost sinner. We would be left with Christ as a failing Mediator who provides a redemption that does not actually redeem. I hesitate to even write those words, such is the scandal of them. But this is what we are left with if "all men" means everyone.

Christ is far more than a hypothetical Savior. Instead, He fulfills the original prophecy of Matthew 1:21, when the angel told Joseph, "You shall call his name Jesus, for he will save his people from their sins."

Just as Christ in His High Priestly prayer made it clear that He was petitioning the Father for a distinct people and not the whole world—"I am praying for them. I am not praying for the world but for those whom you have given me, for they are yours." (John 17:9)—so He died (the very next day) in order to save them. Those He prayed for are the exact same people He died for, and the exact same people He is Mediating for now, in the presence of God. He is the perfect High Priest, the perfect Savior and the perfect Mediator on behalf of His people.

Turning to another Scripture in Revelation chapter 5, we are given prophetic insight into the future, revealing to us what Jesus the Lamb actually achieved in His atoning work on the cross. He did not save everybody or make a mere potential atonement available for everyone. He made an effectual atonement—a powerful one that achieved its desired end or goal of saving certain specific people. What exactly did He achieve?

In Revelation 5:9, the Heavenly anthems ring out in praise of the Lamb saying, for "you were slain, and by your blood you ransomed (specific, actual) people for God from every tribe and language and people and nation..." Note the very specific words used here in this verse. It does not say that Jesus ransomed the people OF, but people FROM, every tribe and language and people and nation. The Greek word for "from" is "*ek*," meaning "out of." He redeemed people *out of* every tribe, language, people group and nation; not all without exception, but all without distinction.

I mention this passage in Revelation 5 because this is in perfect harmony with 1 Timothy 2:4, which very clearly teaches that God desires all (all kinds of people) to be saved and to come to the knowledge of the truth. God will have every tribe, tongue, people group and nation represented around the throne as the heavenly host sing of the Lamb who was slain to redeem them. Hallelujah! What a Savior!

CHAPTER 11

WHAT ABOUT MATTHEW 23:37?

As you may be finding after grappling with the contents of this book, traditions can be very strong. This truth is perhaps never more reflected than in how this particular verse is usually interpreted.

I recently asked an adult group to turn to Matthew 23:37 in their own Bibles and follow along with me. I told them to listen to my words while reading the text in front of them. I asked them to pay close attention to my words because I alerted them ahead of time that I would be omitting two important words from the text while I read it out loud. I told them that I wished to see if they could identify which two words I was omitting.

I read the verse out loud as follows:

"O Jerusalem, Jerusalem, the city that kills the prophets and stones those who are sent to it! How often would I have gathered you together as a hen gathers her brood under her wings, and you would not!"

There was silence from the group.

Then I repeated the process. As I completed the second reading I looked and saw heads buried in their Bibles, but no one spoke up. No one said a word.

I waited another 20 seconds and then said "alright, let me read it again," and repeated the process.

What happened next?

Well, even when telling them to watch out for my intentional omission, it was only after my fourth reading through of the verse that one individual raised their hand to indicate they had the correct answer. Fourth time through one of the adults spotted the fact that I had omitted the words "your children" from the reading.

I acknowledged the correct answer and then read the text the way it actually reads in the Bible, this time emphasizing the words I had previously failed to include.

Matthew 23:37 actually reads:

"O Jerusalem, Jerusalem, the city that kills the prophets and stones those who are sent to it! How often would I have gathered YOUR CHILDREN together as a hen gathers her brood under her wings, and you would not!"

What difference does this all make? All the difference in the world, as I will seek to explain.

Why did I conduct this exercise?

The answer is quite simple. I wanted them to become aware of the power of tradition. It is so powerful that even with warning ahead of time, we often read the text the way we have always interpreted the text rather than by allowing the words to speak for themselves. In this short but powerful exercise, I read the text the way people have understood the text by tradition, not the way the text actually reads. And the omission of the two words changes the interpretation entirely.

Most people assume four things about the text:

(1) Jesus wanted to save the Jews He was speaking to.

(2) Though He desired to do this, He could not.

(3) The reason for this was their stubborn refusal to allow themselves to be gathered. (Christ "would," but they "would not.")

(4) The conclusion: For the grace of God to achieve its objective in the salvation of souls, it is dependent upon the will of man. In spite of all the wooing and drawing desires and actions of God, God's grace can never overcome the stubborn will of man unless man chooses to cooperate. God is often times left frustrated. Christ really tried His best to gather these people, even to the point of tears. But in the end, man's resistance thwarted His will.

What I say now may shock you, but none of those four assumptions is true.

When we look at the text we find that the context of the passage is that Jesus is proclaiming judgment upon the Jewish leaders. It would be fair to say that in this chapter Jesus gives His strongest words of condemnation of the Pharisees and scribes found anywhere in the four Gospels.

The question we should be asking concerns the identity of "Jerusalem" here in the text. Many assume that the term refers to all the individual Jews in the city. But is that a valid interpretation?

The context shows Jesus aiming His speech at the Jewish leaders. God had sent His prophets to them and they (the leaders) had killed them. Jesus then makes a differentiation between the people He is addressing and "your children," whom He sought to gather. "Jerusalem" then refers to the religious leaders of the city.

I hope you can see this. The people the Lord wished to gather are not the same people who were "not willing." No, Jesus is condemning the religious leaders and saying that He desired to gather their children (those under their spiritual care). But they (the leaders) were not willing. The leaders did all in their power to stand in the way of Jesus gathering those He wished to gather. They had cast doubt on Jesus' character and said that His miracles were performed by means of demonic power. And they threatened anyone who confessed Jesus as the Messiah with expulsion from the synagogue!

This is the exact same issue that He raised just a few verses earlier (v. 13) where He said, "But woe to you, scribes and Pharisees, hypocrites! For you shut the kingdom of heaven in people's faces. For you neither enter yourselves nor allow those who would enter to go in."

In all the Synoptic Gospels (Matthew, Mark and Luke) Christ's words of condemnation are faithfully reported. In Matt. 18:6, Mark 9:42 and Luke 17:2 we see Christ's words of censure where He says (almost word for word) "It would be better for him if a millstone were hung around his neck and he were cast into the sea than that he should cause one of these little ones to sin." These leaders were the very ones who should have helped those under their spiritual care to recognize Messiah when He came. They should have led the parade in terms of announcing the joyous news that the long awaited One had come. Instead, they stood opposed to Him and sought even to kill Him. Therefore their guilt was immense in the sight of God.

Matthew 23:37 does not speak to the issue of election or whether or not God's grace is irresistible to the elect. That is a total misreading of the text. Instead it is Christ's word of condemnation to the scribes and Pharisees in Jerusalem: "I sought to gather your children but you were not willing." Therefore woe to you!

One final word before we move on. Someone might raise an objection by saying, "So, its agreed that Jesus sought to gather the children and the spiritual fathers in the city would have none of it. Therefore isn't it plain that God's will was dashed, not by the children's will, but by the leader's will, and does it not follow that God's will to save can indeed be thwarted?"

All I can say to that is "No, it does not mean that at all." That argument can in no way be substantiated by the text. That's because the issue of whether or not Jesus failed to gather is simply not addressed. You have to be engaged in total eisegesis (reading something into the text) to come up with this idea. This concept is not only NOT explicitly stated, I would go further and say that it is NOT implicitly stated either.

What the text teaches us is that Christ desired to gather the leader's children and the leaders were not willing for this to happen, which is why they were under the just condemnation of God. The text says absolutely nothing concerning whether or not Jesus failed to gather the children He desired. Nothing at all!

We should base our thinking on the clear explicit statements in Scripture—things that are derived exegetically (out from the text of Scripture). Concerning this question, Jesus spoke in very clear terms when He said explicitly, "All that the Father gives me will come to me..." (John 6:37). What a comfort that is. He said "all" - not "some," and not "most," but ALL that the Father gives me will come to me.

CHAPTER 12

WHAT ABOUT 1 TIMOTHY 4:10?

This is a verse which is often raised as an objection to God's Sovereignty in election.

"For to this end we toil and strive, because we have our hope set on the living God, who is the Savior of all people, especially of those who believe."

It has had many interpretations. Here are a few of them:

(1) UNIVERSALISM—Universalists interpret the phrase that God is "the Savior of all people" to mean that all will be saved. This is contrary to all sound doctrine and, in fact, has always been viewed as heresy by the Church. The proponents of this idea emphasize the love of God as God's chief and most important attribute, to the exclusion of all others, such as His holiness and His justice. This heresy is very easily refuted because the Bible makes it very clear that some people will end up in hell, forever. (Rev. 14: 9-11; 20:15; Matt. 5: 21-22, 27-30; 23: 15, 33; 25: 41, 46)

If the phrase "the Savior of all people" was seeking to teach universalism, the rest of the verse would have no meaning when it says "especially of those who believe."

(2) ARMINIANISM—Arminians would normally interpret the verse to say that God wants to save everyone but His desire is many times thwarted by the obstinate free will of man. Note though that the passage does not say He wants to save, but that He actually saves: He is actually the Savior (in some sense at least) of all people, not merely a potential Savior.

Also, according to Isaiah 46:10, God's will is never frustrated. He accomplishes all He sets out to do.

(3) A VARIATION OF ARMINIANISM - God is able to save all people, but though all can be saved, only believers actually are. Again, this is not what the text says.

(4) THE REFORMED VIEW—God is the Savior of all people (in one sense) and especially of those who believe (in another sense). Why would this be considered the correct interpretation?

Well, as we study the terms "salvation" and "Savior" in the Bible we find many nuances—many different ways God saves. The most important aspect of salvation is to be "saved" from the wrath of God (Rom. 5:6-9), but salvation also includes the idea of rescue from enemy attack (Psalm 18:3); preservation (Matt. 8:25); physical healing (Matt. 9:22; James 5:15) etc. God "saved" not only Paul but everyone else on board ship with him in Acts 27:22, 31, 44. There are numerous ways that "salvation" takes place, but that's a complete Bible study all in itself.

When we study the word Savior (Greek: soter) in the LXX version (Greek translation of the Old Testament) we see the word used in a way that is far less grandiose than that which we generally think of the word. One example is Judge Othniel is called a Soter (Savior) or deliverer because he delivered the children of Israel from the hands of the king of Mesopotamia (Judg. 3:9). 2 Kings 13:5 talks of God giving Israel a "Savior" so that they were delivered from the hands of the Syrians. The judges of Israel were "saviors" as Nehemiah 9:27 states, "… in the time of their suffering they cried out to you and you heard them from heaven, and according to your great mercies you gave them saviors who saved them from the hand of their enemies." (see also Psalm 36:6).

A great deal more could be said to substantiate this idea of a savior, but I think the above makes the point. God provides food (Psalm 104:27, 28) sunlight and rainfall (Matt. 5:45), as well as life and breath and all things (Acts 17:25), for "In him we live and move and have our being." (Acts 17:28).

God preserves, delivers and supplies the needs of all who live in this world, and it is in this sense that He extends grace to them, saving them from destruction every day they live. God is also gracious in allowing many to hear the proclamation of the Gospel.

All of these mercies are referred to as "common grace." As I pointed out in the chapter "The Place to Start: Amazed by Common Grace" it is common only in the sense that every living person gets it. This grace should actually shock and amaze us because God is under no obligation whatsoever to give it to anyone. God sustains the lives of His sworn enemies, often for many decades! However, as wonderful as it is, it is only a temporal grace because all unregenerate people eventually die and will face the judgment. (Heb. 9:27)

I believe then that 1 Timothy 4:10 teaches that God is the Savior (soter—preserver, sustainer and deliverer) of all people (showing mercy to all, each and every day they live), especially of those who believe (who receive full salvation from His wrath and everlasting life).

CHAPTER 13

WHAT ABOUT JOHN 12:32?

In an earlier chapter there was a brief discussion of John 6:35-45. In that passage, Jesus' teaching could be summarized as follows:

Unless it is granted, no one will come to Christ. All to whom it is granted will be drawn to Christ and come to Christ, and all of these will be raised up to eternal life on the last day.

So, this being the case, what is the meaning of John 12:32, where Jesus said: "And I, when I am lifted up from the earth, will draw all people to myself."

What I will say here may surprise you, but as I have sought to explain elsewhere, the word "all" has a number of different meanings in the Bible. We tend to assume that when Jesus speaks of drawing "all people," He is referring to every last person on the planet. Well, that may or may not be true, but it is in the CONTEXT where we find the phrase that tells us if this assumption is correct or misplaced.

Even today we use the words "all" or "every" in many different ways. When a teacher in a classroom of people asks, "Are we all here?" or "Is everyone listening?" we understand he is not talking about every one of the 7 billion plus folk on the planet, but all the students who have signed up for the class. Context determines the proper interpretation or meaning of words. When the word "all" is used, it is used within a context.

In this illustration, the "all" had a context of the school classroom, which did not include "all" the hockey players in Iceland, "all" the dentists in Denmark, or "all" the carpet layers in Atlanta, Georgia. To rip the word "all" out of its setting and say that the teacher was referring to all people everywhere, would be to totally misunderstand and misinterpret how the word was being used. Again, it is context that determines correct interpretation.

So how do we understand the nature of the drawing in John 12:32? Who exactly is being drawn?

We find answers to these questions by refusing to be lazy, doing some serious study, and by consciously allowing our traditions to be exposed to the light of Scripture.

So if understanding the context plays such a major role in getting the correct interpretation, exactly what is the context of John 12? Well it is a very different setting than the one we find in John 6. In John 12, Greeks (or Gentiles) were coming to Jesus and believing in Him.

John 12:20-22—Now among those who went up to worship at the feast were some Greeks. So these came to Philip, who was from Bethsaida in Galilee, and asked him, "Sir, we wish to see Jesus." Philip went and told Andrew; Andrew and Philip went and told Jesus.

Dr. James White, in his book *The Potter's Freedom* (p. 163), describes the background as follows:

John 12 narrates the final events of Jesus' public ministry. After this particular incident, the Lord will go into a period of private ministry to His disciples right before He goes to the cross. The final words of Jesus' public teachings are prompted by the arrival of Greeks who are seeking Jesus. This important turn of events prompts the teaching that follows. Jesus is now being sought by non-Jews, Gentiles. It is when Jesus is informed of this that He says, "The hour has come for the Son of Man to be glorified." This then is the context which leads us to Jesus' words in verse 32:

John 12:27-33 "Now is my soul troubled. And what shall I say? 'Father, save me from this hour'? But for this purpose I have come to this hour. Father, glorify your name." Then a voice came from heaven: "I have glorified it, and I will glorify it again." The crowd that stood there and heard it said that it had thundered. Others said, "An angel has spoken to him." Jesus answered, "This voice has come for your sake, not mine. Now is the judgment of this world; now will the ruler of this world be cast out. And I, when I am lifted up from the earth, will draw all people to myself." He said this to show by what kind of death he was going to die.

I believe that in its context the "all people" refers to Jews and Gentiles, not to every individual person on earth. Through His work on the cross, Jesus will draw all kinds of men, all kinds of people to Himself, including those from outside of the covenant community of Israel. We must bear in mind that this would have been an extremely radical thought to the Jews who were hearing Him say these words.

FOOLISHNESS OR STUMBLING BLOCK?

But let us look at this issue from another angle by asking the question, "Is it true that everyone on earth is drawn to the cross?" Is that what the Bible really teaches about the cross?

What does the Scripture say? It says that the cross is foolishness to Gentiles and a stumbling block to Jews. 1 Corinthians 1:22-24 says, "For Jews demand signs and Greeks seek wisdom, but we preach Christ crucified, a stumbling block to Jews and folly to Gentiles, but to those who are called, both Jews and Greeks, Christ the power of God and the wisdom of God."

Question: Who views the cross as something other than foolishness or a stumbling block?

Answer: "...those who are called, both Jews and Greeks..." ("Greeks" being a synonym for Gentiles, in this context)

Again, to quote Dr. White:

To whom is Christ the power and wisdom of God? To "the called." What is the preaching of the cross to those who are not called? Something that draws them or repels them? The answer I think is obvious. The cross of Christ is foolishness to the world. These considerations, along with the immediate context of the Gentiles seeking Christ, make it clear that if He is lifted up in crucifixion, He will draw all men, Jews and Gentiles, to Himself. This is exactly the same as saying that He has sheep not of this fold (John 10:16), the Gentiles, who become one body in Christ (Eph. 2:13-16).

If we assume that God is drawing every single individual on the planet we run into a major problem when we use this interpretation of John 12:32 (out of its context) and to try to understand the drawing in John 6:44 in the light of it.

Let us also bear in mind that we would need to demonstrate that the simple word "draw" MUST have the exact same meaning and objects in both contexts—something I don't believe bears out at all.

What is the problem?

Well, if we do this, we end up with the unbiblical doctrine of universalism (all people will be saved).

Why? Because Jesus said in John 6:44: "No one can come to me unless the Father who sent me draws him. And I will raise him up on the last day." The one drawn here is raised up to eternal life. If everyone on the planet is drawn, then all will be saved, which, I am sure you will agree is not a biblical position, for Scripture teaches clearly that not everyone will inherit eternal life.

Rather than solving the issue, this interpretation causes severe problems and in fact undermines the truth of the Gospel. I believe we therefore need to discard this assumption, and interpret both passages in their biblical context. The result will be a consistent revelation of the Sovereign purposes of God in drawing His elect to Himself, for His own purposes, Jews as well as Gentiles, from every tribe, tongue, people and nation.

CHAPTER 14

WHAT ABOUT REPROBATION?

The 16th Century was famous for at least two monumental events: The Protestant Reformation and the Copernican Revolution. No doubt, you have heard of the Reformation when men such as Martin Luther were raised up by God to bring the one true biblical gospel back to the Church. With the Protestant Reformers of old and with Scripture alone as our sure foundation, we affirm that justification is by grace alone, through faith alone, because of Christ alone, to the glory of God alone.

In 1543, Nicolas Copernicus published his treatise *De Revolutionibus Orbium Coelestium* (The Revolution of Celestial Spheres) where a new view of the world was presented: the heliocentric (sun central) model. Before Copernicus, people believed that the earth was the very center of the Universe. But Copernicus was able to prove otherwise—that it is the sun (not the earth) that is central in the solar system. This discovery shook both the religious and the scientific world. The ramifications were extremely dramatic. Our view of the world was forever changed!

Copernicus' theory was not at all popular initially. Even though the new treatise was dedicated to the Pope, it was considered heretical both by the standards of religion and science. Such was the outrage at such a thought (that the world was not the center of the Universe) that many scientists, and sadly, even many a theologian, would not even look through Copernicus' telescope! The traditions of men, both in the realms of science and religion, were that strong.

Yet Copernicus was right and his revolutionary idea was needed if forward progress was to be made. In the Church today, I believe a similar revolution is needed.

What was recognized by former generations, has, by and large, been lost to the modern day Church. The biblical Gospel is rarely heralded. Oh, there are some elements still there. But the facts of the Gospel are presented in man-centered rather than God-centered packaging. One of the most pressing needs in this hour is for the Church to actually be re-evangelized! We, the Church, need to hear a Biblically-based, God-centered, Christ-centered Gospel. We need to hear of God as He really is, of man as he really is, and the Gospel of God's grace found in Jesus Christ as it really is. And all of this starts by understanding that God is at the center and not us.

The natural man is so hostile towards God that if he could kill God, he would, even if it meant the end of his own existence. He also hates the fact that God is Sovereign. When I speak of God's Sovereignty, I mean that God does what He wants, when He wants, the way He wants, without asking anyone's permission.

Jonathan Edwards recalled his own experience:

From my childhood up, my mind had been full of objections against the doctrine of God's sovereignty. It used to appear like a horrible doctrine to me. But I remember the time very well, when I seemed to be convinced, and fully satisfied, as to this sovereignty of God, and His justice in thus eternally dealing with men, according to His sovereign pleasure. My mind rested in it; and it put an end to all those quibbles and objections. And there has been a wonderful alteration in my mind, with respect to the doctrine of God's sovereignty, from that day to this. God's absolute sovereignty is what my mind seems to rest assured of, as much as of anything that I see with my eyes. But I have often, since that first conviction, had quite another kind of sense of God's sovereignty than I had then. I have often since had not only a conviction, but a delightful conviction. The doctrine has appeared exceedingly pleasant, bright, and sweet. Absolute sovereignty is what I love to ascribe to God. But my first conviction was not so. (Memoirs of Jonathan Edwards)

Elsewhere, he wrote:

When men are fallen, and become sinful, God by His sovereignty has a right to determine about their redemption as He pleases. He has a right to determine whether He will redeem any or not. He might, if he had pleased, have left all to perish, or might have redeemed all. Or, he may redeem some, and leave others; and if He doth so, He may take whom He pleases, and leave whom He pleases. To suppose that all have forfeited his favor, and deserved to perish, and to suppose that he may not leave any one individual of them to perish, implies a contradiction; because it supposes that such a one has a claim to God's favor, and is not justly liable to perish; which is contrary to the supposition. It is meet (right) that God should order all these things according to His own pleasure. By reason of His greatness and glory, by which He is infinitely above all, He is worthy to be Sovereign, and that His pleasure should in all things take place. He is worthy that He should make Himself His end, and that He should make nothing but His own wisdom His rule in pursuing that end, without asking leave or counsel of any, and without giving account of any of His matters. It is fit that He who is absolutely perfect, and infinitely wise, and the Fountain of all wisdom, should determine everything [that He effects] by His own will, even things of the greatest importance. It is meet that He should be thus Sovereign, because He is the first being, the eternal being, whence all other beings are. He is the Creator of all things; and all are absolutely and universally dependent on Him; and therefore it is meet that He should act as the Sovereign possessor of heaven and earth. (The Justice of God in the damnation of sinners)

C. H. Spurgeon preached:

There is no attribute of God more comforting to his children than the doctrine of Divine Sovereignty. Under the most adverse circumstances, in the most severe troubles, they believe that Sovereignty hath ordained their afflictions, that Sovereignty overrules them, and that Sovereignty will sanctify them all. There is nothing for which the children of God ought more earnestly to contend than the dominion of their Master over all creation—the kingship of God over all the works of His own hands—the throne of God, and His right to sit upon that throne. On the other hand, there is no doctrine more hated by world-lings, no truth of which they have made such a football, as the great, stupendous, but yet most certain doctrine of the Sovereignty of the infinite Jehovah. Men will allow God to be everywhere except on His throne. (Sermon "Divine Sovereignty," from May 4, 1856, at New Park Street Chapel, Southwark)

In Isaiah 46:8-10, God declares, "Remember this and stand firm, recall it to mind, you transgressors, remember the former things of old; for I am God, and there is no other; I am God, and there is none like me, declaring the end from the beginning and from ancient times things not yet done, saying, 'My counsel shall stand, and I will accomplish all my purpose.'" God achieves all He sets out to accomplish. His plans are never thwarted or frustrated.

The natural man does not have a mere distaste for this idea; he hates it with a vengeance. As J. C. Ryle has said, *Of all the doctrines of the Bible, none is so offensive to human nature as the doctrine of God's Sovereignty. (Commentary on Luke 4:22-32, source gracegems.org)*

Man wants the control. He wants to be in charge of his own destiny. He hates to admit the fact that God is on the throne and one day he will answer to Him. Even more than this, that hates that he is powerless to prevent God's ultimate purpose being achieved. The idea is repugnant to "autonomous" man, governed, he thinks, by his own free will.

In spite of this, the fact is that God is in charge. Man is not the center of the Universe, God is! It is time for the church to once again sound out the truth! "For from him and through him and to him are all things. To him be glory forever. Amen." (Rom. 11:36).God "works all things according to the counsel of his will" (Eph 1:11).

Just as mankind had to adjust to Copernicus' discovery, we need to adjust our thinking to the facts of Scripture. God is Sovereign. That's just the way it is! God is Sovereign in all things, including how He dispenses His grace. The Reformers declared "Sola Gratia" (Grace Alone), and by that declaration they meant grace at the start, grace to the end, grace in the middle, grace without fail, grace without mixture, grace without addition, grace that allows no boasting, grace that precludes all glorying but in the Lord. Just as many refused to look through Copernicus' telescope in his day, many refuse to look at the Scriptures in ours. Let that not be true of you and me.

When it comes to reprobation, there is no doubt that this is a highly-charged, emotional question, not merely an intellectual one. So much so that it is hard for any of us to consider this issue with any degree of objectivity. That is because we are talking about real people facing an eternity of severe punishment under the hand of God's judgment. It is an extremely difficult question for any of us to handle emotionally.

Having said that, let us at least try to look at this issue through a biblical lens (what the Bible reveals to us).

Here is what we know. All Bible believing Christians would affirm that God knows the end from the beginning and therefore has exhaustive knowledge of the future. Therefore, He creates people whom He knows will end up in hell. There is no way to avoid this conclusion.

God does indeed know His sheep and He knows those who are not (see John 10:25,26) and there are indeed Scriptures that talk of predestination to reprobation—just one being 1 Peter 2:8, "They stumble because they disobey the word, as they were destined to do."

In contrast, those who believe were predestined by God. Acts 13:48 says, "And when the Gentiles heard this, they began rejoicing and glorifying the word of the Lord, and as many as were appointed to eternal life believed."

Concerning the beast of Revelation we are told, "All that dwell on the earth shall worship him, every one whose name hath not been written from the foundation of the world in the book of life of the lamb that hath been slain" (Rev. 13:8).

This verse alone is enough to settle the matter. God knows the identity of those who will worship the Beast (and therefore go to a lost eternity) and He knew this before the world was ever made.

Once again we can contrast these with the disciples whom Jesus told to rejoice because their names were written in heaven (Luke 10:20), and with those who worked alongside the Apostle Paul, "whose names are in the book of life" (Phil. 4:3).

Indeed, there is a flip side to the doctrine of Divine election; that being reprobation. Here is an excerpt from Loraine Boettner's book "The Reformed Doctrine of Predestination":

Christ's command to the wicked in the final judgment, "Depart from me, ye cursed, into the eternal fire which is prepared for the Devil and his angels," Matt. 25:41, is the strongest possible decree of reprobation; and it is the same in principle whether issued in time or eternity. What is right for God to do in time it is not wrong for Him to include in His eternal plan.

On one occasion Jesus Himself declared: "For judgment came I into this world, that they that see not may see; and that they that see may become blind," John 9:39. On another occasion He said, "I thank thee, O Father, Lord of heaven and earth, that thou didst hide these things from the wise and understanding, and didst reveal them unto babes," Matt. 11:25.

It is hard for us to realize that the adorable Redeemer and only Savior of men is, to some, a stone of stumbling and a rock of offence; yet that is what the Scriptures declare Him to be. Even before His birth it was said that He was set (that is, appointed) for the falling, as well as for the rising, of many in Israel (Luke 2:34). And when, in His intercessory prayer in the garden of Gethsemane, He said, "I pray for them; I pray not for the world, but for those whom thou hast given me," the non-elect were repudiated in so many words.

Jesus Himself declared that one of the reasons why He spoke in parables was that the truth might be concealed from those for whom it was not intended. We shall let the sacred history speak for itself: "And the disciples came, and said unto Him, Why speakest thou unto them in parables? And He answered and said unto them, Unto you it is given to know the mysteries of the kingdom of heaven, but unto them it is not given. For whosoever hath, to him shall be given, and he shall have abundance; but whosoever hath not, from him shall be taken away even that which he hath. Therefore speak I unto them in parables; because seeing they see not, and hearing they hear not, neither do they understand. And unto them is fulfilled the prophecy of Isaiah, which saith,

"By hearing ye shall hear, and shall in no wise understand;
And seeing ye shall see, and shall in no wise perceive;
For this people's heart is waxed gross.
And their ears are dull of hearing.
And their eyes they have closed;
Lest haply they should perceive with their eyes,
And hear with their ears,
And understand with their heart,
And should turn again,
And I should heal them." Matt. 13:10-15; Is 6:9, 10.

In these words we have an application of Jesus' words, "Give not that which is holy unto the dogs, neither cast your pearls before swine," Matt. 7:6. He who affirms that Christ designed to give His saving truth to everyone flatly contradicts Christ Himself. To the non-elect, the Bible is a sealed book; and only to the true Christian is it "given" to see and understand these things. So important is this truth that the Holy Spirit has been pleased to repeat six times over in the New Testament this passage from Isaiah (Matt. 13:14, 15; Mark 4:12; Luke 8:10; John 12:40; Acts 28:27: Rom. 11:9, 10).

Romans 9 tells us why God would create people knowing their final end will be an eternity in hell—to demonstrate His wrath and make His power known (see the passage below). This never sits well with us when our starting point in the pursuit of truth is man and his feelings, for even as redeemed men and women, we have much more sympathy with fellow sinners than with the holiness and righteousness of God.

Think about that for a moment and I believe it will strike the heart, for we have much more in common even with a Hitler or Stalin, than we do with the holiness, majesty and glory of Almighty God, and this itself is a manifestation of our deep depravity.

BUT if we make the big paradigm shift and see life, the universe and everything from the starting point of the rightness of God being glorified in all His attributes, then everything begins to make perfect sense.

I believe that with minds that are fully sanctified in heaven we will rejoice that God's righteousness is being glorified. But here, our fallenness makes us cringe that a fellow human being, as bad as he may be, may face the judgment of God for all eternity, knowing that God knew this would be where that person would end up even before He created him. This side of heaven it is hard for us to see God's desire to display His attributes such as His righteousness, justice and wrath as a valid reason for God doing what He does. But in heaven, with glorified and sanctified minds, we will not have that problem at all.

I think the following passage in Romans 9 spells it out that it is right for God to show forth His attributes, even in the damnation of "vessels of wrath prepared for destruction" just as He does so through redeeming the "vessels of mercy"— certainly God thinks so:

[14]What shall we say then? Is there injustice on God's part? By no means! [15]For he says to Moses, "I will have mercy on whom I have mercy, and I will have compassion on whom I have

compassion." [16]So then it depends not on human will or exertion, but on God, who has mercy. [17]For the Scripture says to Pharaoh, "For this very purpose I have raised you up, that I might show my power in you, and that my name might be proclaimed in all the earth." [18]So then he has mercy on whomever he wills, and he hardens whomever he wills.

[19]You will say to me then, "Why does he still find fault? For who can resist his will?" [20]But who are you, O man, to answer back to God? Will what is molded say to its molder, "Why have you made me like this?" [21] Has the potter no right over the clay, to make out of the same lump one vessel for honorable use and another for dishonorable use? [22]What if God, desiring to show his wrath and to make known his power, has endured with much patience vessels of wrath prepared for destruction, [23]in order to make known the riches of his glory for vessels of mercy, which he has prepared beforehand for glory— [24]even us whom he has called, not from the Jews only but also from the Gentiles?

For anyone still struggling with this concept, I do understand that you might need much more than a few short words here. However, I would ask you to keep struggling (so to speak) and look through the Scriptures on this issue. I will also point you to further reading material for you to consider at the end of this book.

I know that my own struggle with this concept was not because Scripture is not clear, for indeed it is. My problem was that I did not LIKE what Scripture taught. It did not fit with my preconceptions about God.

In the end I realized that to continue the struggle would be to oppose God Himself. He is the God who inspired Romans 9 and it is to Him we must one day give account. I would hate to be one who defied Him and have to give an account of my continued opposition to Him in the face of His revealed truth.

One further thing: Many people have a false concept of this doctrine which is called "Equal Ultimacy." This false view of reprobation maintains that God does just as much in and to the wicked to cause their damnation as He does in His elect to cause their salvation. This is obviously not the case at all. Though it is true that God "has mercy on whomever he wills, and he hardens whomever he wills," (Rom. 9:18) we need to understand that there are two possible ways God could harden the heart.

In one scenario He could inject fresh evil into the soul of man. Such is an abhorrent thought and one totally opposed to Scripture.

In the other scenario, God could simply leave man in his state of rebellion by withholding the special measure of grace He gives to His elect. Unregenerate man's natural disposition is one of opposition to Him. All He needs to do to harden the heart is withhold the special grace he gives to His elect, leaving them in their evil, prideful, hateful, defiance of Him.

In all this there is not even a trace of injustice taking place. God either dispenses the justice that is deserved or an unspeakable mercy that is underserved. But no one—absolutely no one— receives injustice from the hand of God.

CHAPTER 15

WHAT ABOUT LOST LOVED ONES?

Let me address this question by telling you a story from history.
In the 4th century, there was a very devout Christian lady
named Monica. She was married to a prominent man who did
not share her Christian faith. He was often very cruel to her,
causing her physical abuse. Every day she would go to the
church and pray for his conversion. Later on in his life, he did in
fact become a Christian.

Yet the pain and anguish her husband caused her seemingly
paled into insignificance compared to that which she suffered
because of her oldest son. Her mother's heart was broken, time
after time, seeing the reckless life her son was leading. He not
only did not share his mother's faith but would join himself to
anti-Christian groups, using his sharp mind to seek to convince
others to follow him. He lived a very immoral life. He had a
mistress but left her for another and had a son born out of
wedlock, named Adeodatus. Monica was not personally able to
convince her son of the truth claims of Christianity, but she
determined never to stop praying that he would turn to the Lord.

For two decades this went on, with Monica persisting in prayer
for her son, seemingly seeing no results. Her son was later to
write about all this and tells us that she wept more for his
spiritual death than most mothers weep for the bodily death of
their children. Distraught, she went to see the well known
Bishop Ambrose of Milan to speak about her plight. Knowing

her anguish of soul he said, "Go your way and God will bless you, for it is not possible that the son of these tears should perish." She accepted the answer as though it were a word from God Himself.

Monica's prayers for her son were answered very suddenly. One day he was in a garden experiencing much agony of soul because of his sin. God the Holy Spirit was certainly working on him. In his own writings he recalled what happened next— suddenly he heard the voice of a boy or a girl, he was not sure which, coming from the neighboring house, chanting over and over again, "Tolle Lege, Tolle Lege" a Latin phrase that meant 'Pick it up, read it; pick it up, read it.'

Later, in his own writings, he recounted, *Immediately I ceased weeping and began most earnestly to think whether it was usual for children in some kind of game to sing such a song, but I could not remember ever having heard the like. So, damming the torrent of my tears, I got to my feet, for I could not but think that this was a divine command to open the Bible and read the first passage I should light upon....*

So I quickly returned to the bench where Alypius [his friend] was sitting, for there I had put down the apostle's book when I had left there. I snatched it up, opened it, and in silence I read the paragraph on which my eyes first fell: 'Not in rioting and drunkenness, not in chambering and wantonness, not in strife and envying, but put on the Lord Jesus Christ, and make no provision for the flesh to fulfill the lusts thereof' (Rom. 13:13). I wanted to read no further, nor did I need to. For instantly, as the sentence ended, there was infused in my heart something like the light of full certainty and all the gloom of doubt vanished away. - Augustine, 'Confessions', VIII.12.29

Monica's many years of prayers were answered in a single moment. Her son experienced a dramatic, life changing conversion to Christ.

What Monica could not have known was the impact her son would have, not only on his contemporaries, but on the many generations to come. Her son became one of God's greatest ever gifts to His Church, Augustine of Hippo (354 AD to 430 AD). There is no doubt that Augustine was the greatest theologian of the Church (outside of the New Testament) for the first thousand years, and arguably, he was the greatest theologian in Church history. Augustine's writings on the subject of grace would become a massive influence on both Martin Luther (who was himself an Augustinian monk) and John Calvin. God used these men to bring about the greatest move of God in the history of the Church as entire nations were brought under the influence of the gospel in the 16th century Protestant Reformation.

In the same way, as we consider the biblical story of the man who found Christ right at the end of his life, the man known as "the thief on the cross," we should note that even up until the very last day in this man's life, there was nothing we could observe outwardly that would indicate he was one of God's elect. Until this time, the man had lived the life of a notorious criminal with seemingly no interest in following Christ. The fact that he was indeed one of God's elect only became clear when he came to Christ so shortly before death.

While hanging on a cross next to Jesus, he turned to Him and said, "Jesus, remember me when you come into your kingdom." (Luke 23:42).

Immediately, upon speaking these words, this man was given the unique and unspeakably gracious privilege of being told by Jesus Himself that he would be with Him in Paradise that very day (v. 43). What clear words of assurance! If ever a man could be certain of his election, it was this man.

Yet, using our sanctified minds, perhaps we could imagine his mother as a Christian and praying for him as a wayward son. This is complete speculation of course—but let us for a moment suppose that his mother was still alive, a follower of Christ, and was witnessing the events of that day. There would have been nothing that she could have observed with her senses that would have indicated that the last hour of his life would mean his conversion. It looked like it was going to be a tragic end to a tragic life. I certainly could imagine her bitterly intense sorrow in seeing her son walk the same hill as the Savior, the difference being that her son was walking up the hill because he deserved it... and then, out of nowhere it would seem, God the Holy Spirit moved in invisible but irresistible grace and took out the spiritual heart of stone and gave him a new heart, with new affections so unlike the old ones. Immediately, her son trusted in the work of the One dying next to him. And in no time at all, ultimate assurance was given to him that the day would not be over before he would be with Christ in Paradise. As I say, this is all speculation concerning his mother and her anguish of heart, but what is indeed certain is that the man was converted with just hours to go before he died. Absolutely no one is beyond God's reach, even to the last moment of a person's life. Praise the Lord!

The Scripture tells us, "The Lord knows those who are his..." (2 Tim. 2:19).The identity of the elect is known only to God, not to us. Only upon seeing someone defy God until their very last breath in this world should we assume someone is non-elect. Though the salvation of our children or loved ones is always in God's hands, it should be an immense comfort to us knowing that if an individual's conversion is so much upon our hearts, this in itself is a very strong indication that it is God

Himself who is behind the whole thing and has laid this burden upon us, in order that He would use this (our burden to pray) as a *means* to accomplish His *ends* (the conversion of one of His elect sheep). Just as the Lord opened up the heart of Lydia to respond to the things spoken by Paul (Acts 16:13,14), so our only hope is that the God who can open any heart will do so for the ones we love and care for. Salvation (and the timing of conversion) is of the Lord (Jonah 2:9).

CHAPTER 16

WHAT ABOUT PRAYER AND EVANGELISM?

The question is often asked this way: If God elects certain people to salvation what would be the point of prayer and evangelism?

The issue of prayer was discussed somewhat in the last chapter, so allow me to focus my answer on the "evangelism" element in the question here.

When I am asked this, I usually start by altering the wording of the question. I would change the word "if" to "since." Here's what I mean. In that Divine election is clearly taught in Scripture, it would be better to ask, "Since God elects certain people to salvation, why are we told to evangelize?"

The first obvious answer to this question is: Because God tells us to. The same Bible that teaches Divine Sovereign Election in Romans chapters 8 and 9, also gives us Romans 10, saying, "How shall they hear without a preacher?" Romans 10 is in no way a contradiction to Romans 8 and 9.

God ordains both the *ends* and the *means*. The end is His elect coming to saving faith. The means is: The proclamation of the Gospel.

In John 10:16, Jesus said, "And I have other sheep that are not of this fold. I must bring them also, and they will listen to my voice. So there will be one flock, one shepherd."

Jesus already has Jewish sheep. Yet He knows He has other sheep "not of this fold" (a reference to Gentiles). These will listen to His voice. The end is: Elect Gentiles coming into the kingdom. The means is: Jesus' preaching and teaching.

In Matthew chapter 11, we once again see Jesus grounding evangelism in election and once again there is no contradiction between the two...

Matthew 11: 25 At that time Jesus declared, "I thank you, Father, Lord of heaven and earth, that you have hidden these things from the wise and understanding and revealed them to little children; 26 yes, Father, for such was your gracious will. 27 All things have been handed over to me by my Father, and no one knows the Son except the Father, and no one knows the Father except the Son and anyone to whom the Son chooses to reveal him. 28 Come to me, all who labor and are heavy laden, and I will give you rest. 29 Take my yoke upon you, and learn from me, for I am gentle and lowly in heart, and you will find rest for your souls. 30 For my yoke is easy, and my burden is light."

Notice that Jesus teaches us:
(1) God hides things from some and reveals them to others (Sovereign election)
(2) The evangelistic call goes out to all—"Come to me, all..."

For decades I had read these words but I think what I had done before was see verses 25-27 which speak of God's Sovereignty in election, as unrelated to the following words in the text, verse 28, where Jesus invites all to come to Him. Now I see they are said in the same breath, so to speak, and of course, there's no contradiction whatsoever.

Notice also the experience of the early Apostles in Acts 13:
[43]And after the meeting of the synagogue broke up, many Jews and devout converts to Judaism followed Paul and Barnabas,

who, as they spoke with them, urged them to continue in the grace of God. [44]The next Sabbath almost the whole city gathered to hear the word of the Lord. [45] But when the Jews saw the crowds, they were filled with jealousy and began to contradict what was spoken by Paul, reviling him. [46]And Paul and Barnabas spoke out boldly, saying, "It was necessary that the word of God be spoken first to you. Since you thrust it aside and judge yourselves unworthy of eternal life, behold, we are turning to the Gentiles. [47] For so the Lord has commanded us, saying, "'I have made you a light for the Gentiles, that you may bring salvation to the ends of the earth.'" [48]And when the Gentiles heard this, they began rejoicing and glorifying the word of the Lord, and as many as were appointed to eternal life believed.

In an earlier chapter, verse 48 was quoted to show that the ones who believed were appointed by God to do so. Now I quote the greater context to show the simple concept that God ordained both the end (the elect coming to faith) and the means (the preaching of the Gospel).

We should also note how the Lord spoke to the Apostle Paul, in the middle of an intense situation, telling him to stay in a certain city. Why was this? Well let's read the text in Acts 18:
[9]And the Lord said to Paul one night in a vision, "Do not be afraid, but go on speaking and do not be silent, [10] for I am with you, and no one will attack you to harm you, for I have many in this city who are my people."
[11]And he stayed a year and six months, teaching the word of God among them.

In other words, the Lord said to Paul, "Stay here, for I have many people in this city... I have many of My sheep here that will hear My voice and follow Me as you preach in My Name."

God ordains both the end—His chosen sheep who will hear Christ's voice—and the means—prayer, and the preaching of the Gospel to all. And all who are ordained to eternal life will believe.

The fact is, we do not know who the elect are. They are not walking around the countryside with the letter "E" for Elect stamped upon their foreheads. We are therefore to go into all the world and preach the Gospel to everyone, even though we know ahead of time that only His elect will respond in faith to the preaching of the Gospel.

Without election, evangelism would be much like a salesman trying to sell his products in a graveyard. Mankind is spiritually dead in trespasses and sins (Eph. 2:1), and only through the gracious act of God in electing, predestinating, and regenerating a specific people, will anyone ever turn to Christ. As Dr. R. C. Sproul wrote: *If the final decision for the salvation of fallen sinners were left in the hands of fallen sinners, we would despair all hope that anyone would be saved. (Chosen by God)* Again, God ordains both the ends and the means, and the means are just as much ordained by God as the ends. Prayer and evangelism are vital components of the means.

A.A. Hodge once asked: *If God has eternally decreed that you should live, what is the use of your breathing? If God has eternally decreed that you should talk, what is the use of your opening your mouth? If God has eternally decreed that you should reap a crop, what is the use of your sowing the seed? If God has eternally decreed that your stomach should contain food, what is the use of your eating?*

Hodge answered his own questions, by saying: *In order to educate us, [God] demands that we should use the means, or go without the ends which depend upon them. There are plenty of fools who make the transcendental nature of eternity and of the relation of the eternal life of God to the time-life of man an excuse for neglecting prayer. But of all the many fools in the*

United States, there is not one absurd enough to make the same eternal decree an excuse for not chewing his food or for not voluntarily inflating his lungs. (Evangelical Theology, p. 92, 93)

I think that's very clear isn't it?

It is also important to point out that our prayers for unbelievers would be useless if God did not have the power to bring someone from spiritual death to life. Those who reject God's sovereignty in salvation are trusting that God cannot really help the unregenerate by giving them a new understanding, for in their way of thinking, this would mean that God is tampering with free will, something He would not do (according to their theological system). So in that way of thinking, when we pray for unbelievers, God can only do something outside of them, (wooing, encouraging, offering grace, etc.). But He can never do anything inside of them (taking out the heart of stone, putting in a heart of flesh with a positive desire for Christ), which, when you think about it, is not very helpful to those who have no desire for God and who are dead in trespasses and sins. In other words, praying for people to come to Christ makes no sense unless God alone opens hearts. Such was the testimony of Lydia, as Luke informs us in Acts 16:14, "The Lord opened her heart to pay attention to what was said by Paul."

WARNING PASSAGES

This principle of ends and means is a very helpful tool when it comes to understanding the numerous warning passages in the New Testament, especially as found in the book of Hebrews. Many people believe they teach that true believers can ultimately lose their salvation However, as Thomas Schreiner states in an online article written 12.29.2011 at credomag.com:

We must remember that the passages are warnings and admonitions. They say nothing about whether believers will actually fall away. They are not declarations but warnings. The common response is that the warnings are beside the point if believers can't fall away. What a silly waste of time! But that objection fails if the warnings are a means by which God keeps his elect. I would argue that the warning passages are always effective in the lives of the elect, i.e., those who are truly saved always heed the warnings, and it is precisely by heeding the warnings that they are preserved until the end.

Returning once again to the theme of this chapter, we can make the following scriptural statements based on what is revealed to us in the Gospel of John:

All that the Father has chosen to be His from eternity, He has given to the Son (John 6:37); and all whom He has given to the Son, the Son knows (John 10:3); and calls (John 10:3-5); and all whom He calls, know Him (John 10:14) and recognize His voice (John 10:4-5) and they come to Him (John 6:37) and follow Him (John 10:4,27); and the Son lays down His life for His sheep (John 10:11); and He gives them eternal life (John 10:28) and keeps them in the Father's word (John 17:6), so that not even one of them is lost (John 6:39), to glorify the Son forever. (John 17:10).This is the indestructible foundation for an infallible salvation that redounds in the end to the glory of both the Father and the Son.

None of Christ's sheep finally reject His word. Though He allows some of His sheep to resist the word for a long time, never do they reject it finally. Jesus said, "All that the Father gives Me will come to Me." (John 6:37).What a promise! And what a privilege we have in sharing the Gospel with people, as we witness the Good Shepherd rounding up His sheep.

Much more could be said. Church history shows that rather than belief in election causing missions work to wane, the exact opposite is true. A case could be made that in the history of the Church, the men most used by God in the cause of evangelism, were passionate believers in God's Sovereign Grace in election.

———

A controversialist once said, "If I thought God had a chosen people, I should not preach." That is the very reason why I do preach. What would make him inactive is the mainspring of my earnestness. If the Lord had not a people to be saved, I should have little to cheer me in the ministry.

I believe that God will save his own elect, and I also believe that, if I do not preach the gospel, the blood of men will be laid at my door. - C. H. Spurgeon (www.spurgeon.us)

I hope we shall catch fire from each other, and that there will be a holy emulation amongst us, who shall most debase man and exalt the Lord Jesus. Nothing but the doctrines of the Reformation can do this. All others leave freewill in man and make him, in part at least, a Saviour to himself. My soul, come not thou near the secret of those who teach such things... I know Christ is all in all. Man is nothing: he hath a free will to go to hell, but none to go to heaven, till God worketh in him to do of His good pleasure. - George Whitefield, Works, pp. 89-90

Oh, the excellency of the doctrine of election and of the saint's final perseverance! I am persuaded, till a man comes to believe and feel these important truths, he cannot come to himself, but when convinced of these, and assured of their application to his own heart, he then walks by faith indeed!... Love, not fear, constrains him to obedience. - George Whitefield, Works, p. 101

CHAPTER 17

SAVING FAITH

The Apostle Paul's main theme in the book of Romans is that of the Gospel itself, as he answers the question, "How can an unjust person ever be acceptable to a just and holy God?" In passages such as Chapter 3:20 to 4:8, he makes it abundantly clear that we are justified (God declaring us right with Him) on the basis of faith alone and not by anything that we do. Other passages where Paul states this are Titus 3:5; Gal. 2:16; Eph. 2:8,9; Phil. 3:9; to name just a few.

Romans 3:28; 4:3-8 declares, "For we hold that one is justified by faith apart from works of the law... For what does the Scripture say? 'Abraham believed God, and it was counted to him as righteousness.' Now to the one who works, his wages are not counted as a gift but as his due. And to the one who does not work but believes in him who justifies the ungodly, his faith is counted as righteousness, just as David also speaks of the blessing of the one to whom God counts righteousness apart from works: 'Blessed are those whose lawless deeds are forgiven, and whose sins are covered; blessed is the man against whom the Lord will not count his sin.'"

Having established the case biblically that we are justified by faith apart from works, we then need to ask the question, "What kind of faith is it that justifies?" In other words, what does genuine, saving faith look like?

A CLAIM IS NOT ENOUGH

This is precisely the issue that James is addressing in chapter 2 of his epistle. He writes in verse 14, "What good is it, my brothers, if someone says he has faith but does not have works? Can that faith save him?"

The obvious answer to James' rhetorical question is "No, that is not the kind of faith that saves. True faith will produce works." It is never enough to merely make a claim to have faith. No one is ever saved by a mere empty profession of faith. What is professed, must actually be possessed for justification to exist.

James teaches us clearly that if genuine faith is present, it necessarily produces the fruit of works. That's the nature of true faith. In fact, if works do not follow from "faith," then it is proof positive that the "faith" is not in fact genuine, but a mere claim to it.

There is no discord between what James writes and what we find in Romans and the rest of Paul's writings. Faith without works is dead, and a dead faith never saved anyone. True faith is a living faith, and will inevitably show itself with accompanying action or works. Yet even if all these good works do come from genuine faith, these works still have no part in the ground of our justification. Our works add no merit to us, removing all grounds for boasting. "For by grace you have been saved through faith. And this is not your own doing; it is the gift of God, not a result of works, so that no one may boast." (Eph. 2:8, 9).

The only work that contributes to our justification is the work of Jesus; not the work of Jesus *in* us, but the work of Jesus *for* us. His merit is the only merit that counts for us. Paul tells us that it we are justified by faith apart from works, and James tells us that that kind of faith that actually saves is a faith that will of necessity produce works.

The Reformers of the 16th Century were very clear about all this. They described true, saving faith as having three components, which were described by three Latin words: *notitia*, *assensus* and *fiducia*.

1. CONTENT OR INFORMATION (*notitia*) - Like our modern day word "notice", notitia concerns information or knowledge of the truth of the gospel. We need to understand the facts of the Gospel.

What exactly must be believed?

Certainly, a person does not need to be a highly trained theologian to be saved. The Holy Spirit draws both adults and young children to a saving knowledge of Christ. Yet when children are converted to Christ, they may not know every nuance of the faith, or even a detailed understanding of the atonement—merely that Christ died for our sins. However, I believe it would be true to say that a truly saved person, although they may not be able to articulate the content of the Gospel at length, will not reject it when they do hear it. I believe that's a very important point to make. Jesus said, "My sheep hear my voice, and I know them, and they follow me. I give them eternal life, and they will never perish." (John 10: 27, 28).Christ's true sheep instinctively know the Shepherd's voice and follow Him. The regenerate person humbly submits to the faithful teaching of Scripture when hearing it (Scripture being the Shepherd's voice), unlike those who are still in the flesh who remain completely incapable of doing so (Romans 8:7, 8).

This noticia includes belief in one God, in the full humanity (1 John 4:3) and deity of Christ (John 8:24), and His death for sinners on the cross (1 Cor. 15:3), as well as His physical resurrection from the dead. Romans 10:9 tells us, "If you confess with your mouth that Jesus is Lord and believe in your heart that God raised him from the dead, you will be saved."

I believe the noticia would also include some understanding of God's grace in salvation — that is, God saves us because of Christ's work on behalf of sinners, not the sinner's work on behalf of God. Dr. James White writes: *God's grace is powerful, and it brings full salvation to the soul of the person who despairs of anything other than free, unmerited grace. Grace cannot clasp the hand that carries within it ideas of merit, or good works, or any other kind of human addition to grace. "But if it is by grace, it is no longer on the basis of works, otherwise grace is no longer grace" (Romans 11:6). God's wondrous grace cannot be mixed with human merit. The hand that holds onto its own alleged goodness, or attempts to sneak in a merit here, a good work there, will not find the open hand of God's grace. Only the empty hand fits into the powerful hand of grace. Only the person who finds in Christ his all-in-all will, in so finding, be made right with God. This is why the Scriptures say it is by faith so that it might be in accordance with grace: in God's wisdom, he excludes man's boasting by making salvation all of grace. (The Empty Hand of Faith, tract)*

2. BELIEF (*assensus*) - It is entirely possible to understand something (the notitia) and yet not believe it personally (assensus). Therefore, we need to be able to say, "I both understand and believe the content of the gospel."

3. COMMITMENT (*fiducia*)—The third component of saving faith is a full trust in and commitment to the One who loved us and died for us. This is of critical importance because it is possible to understand these truths, believe they are true, and yet pull back from the necessary personal commitment that will actually enlist us as one of Christ's followers. To possess only the first two parts (notitia and assensus), without the third part (fiducia), merely qualifies us to be demons! James 2:19 declares, "You believe that God is one; you do well. Even the demons believe—and shudder!" Even demons understand and believe, but that does not mean that they have any share in redemption.

True saving faith will always produce the fruit of good works. That is its nature. Though our works play no part at all in justifying us before God, they justify or vindicate our *claim* to faith before a watching world. Our lives should demonstrate that the faith professed was, and is, also possessed.

As you consider your own standing before God, would you say that yours is based completely upon what the Lord Jesus Christ has done in your place (rather than what you do for Him)? Can you honestly say you trust Him with your eternal destiny, and fully believe He carried your sins on the cross, that He rose again from the dead, and that He indeed is your personal Savior and Lord? Do you believe He has forgiven your sins and given His righteousness to you, so that you can stand justified (declared right in His sight) both now and on the Day of Judgment?

If at the present time you are not able to answer these questions in the affirmative, I pray that God will indeed give you the gift of true repentance and faith, turning away from all attempts at self-righteousness and self-justification and instead transfer all your personal trust to the perfect Savior, the Lord Jesus Christ. Call upon the Name of the Lord and be saved.

CHAPTER 18

THE FLAMING MISSILES OF THE DEVIL

One of the first things God did for me after I had come to faith in Christ was to give me a deep settled assurance of salvation. Romans 8:16 tells us, "The Spirit himself bears witness with our spirit that we are children of God..." This inner witness brought me the sure knowledge that despite my many flaws and failures, I was in fact His; His for all eternity. As I read the Scriptures, the wonders of this great salvation become clear; God had saved me, I was His, and Christ did indeed love me and had given me eternal life. Heaven sent peace flooded my soul. I knew I could say, "I am my Beloved's and He is mine."

But then, somewhere along the way, this settled peace was disturbed. The wonders of His grace, wrought through Christ and His atoning work became obscured... not because I read some book countering the claims of Christianity and was swayed by the arguments, but because I came across Scriptures that at least at first glance, seemed to show that my salvation was a lot more flimsy and shaky than I first imagined. I wonder if you can relate to any of this.

Here's what I mean: I read Scriptures such as "nothing can separate us from the love of God" (Rom. 8: 39) but then read "the one who endures to the end will be saved." (Matt. 24:13)

I read, "...whoever believes in Him will not perish but have eternal life" (John 3:16) and then read "Now I would remind you, brothers, of the gospel I preached to you, which you received, in which you stand, and by which you are being saved, if you hold fast to the word I preached to you—unless you believed in vain." (1 Cor. 15:1,2).

I thought, "which is it God? In one verse it says that if someone believes, they can be certain of eternal life, but in another verse it says that someone can 'believe in vain.' How could both statements be true?"

I read about how God started the work in us and would in fact complete it (Phil. 1:6) and that "these whom He justified, He glorified" (Rom. 8:30) showing me that none of His truly justified saints fall through the cracks, but all end up saved. I cannot for a moment imagine Jesus failing to fulfill the will of His Father, and in John 6:39 He makes it clear what the Father's will actually is: "And this is the will of him who sent me, that I should lose nothing of all that he has given me, but raise it up on the last day."

Scriptures such as these gave me great assurance that I was saved by grace alone through faith alone in Christ alone. But then I read other Scripture verses that would say things such as, "without holiness no one will see the Lord." (Heb. 12:14).

That was a verse that terrified me, plaguing my conscience continually. As holy as my life was compared to what it was before, (I now had a great love of the Scriptures and spent many hours each day studying them, even as a young teenager), I knew I never measured up to even my own standards, let alone God's. If I prayed for 20 minutes, the thought came to me, "If you were a real Christian, you would have prayed longer."

Where did that kind of thought come from?

I knew it was probably the enemy, but I had little with which to fight those thoughts. If I shared my faith with a friend, my conscience would point out to me that there was another guy walking down the street I could have stopped and witnessed to. I could never do enough to assuage my conscience.

I heard sermons where the preacher talked about the difference between conviction of the Holy Spirit and condemnation (which comes from the devil) and although understanding this distinction certainly helped, my conscience still screamed that I was not as holy as I should be. Lurking at the back of my mind was the constant pounding of that haunting Scripture "without holiness, no one will see the Lord." The poisoned lies of the enemy were like fiery darts that assaulted my mind.

The enemy can quote Scripture (Matt. 4:5). Looking back now, I can see that he was taking advantage of my lack of knowledge. The result of this was that Bible verses that were meant to bless, inspire and comfort me, instead became the source of great confusion and anguish of heart.

So what happened to change this ever deepening cycle of despair?

My answer came by doing a lot of thinking. "Thinking?" you might say. That does not seem too spiritual. Perhaps you thought I might say that I had some sort of "experience"—that I went to some conference and experienced a vision of glory—or maybe I was taken up into heaven and given the privilege of seeing my name written in the Lamb's book of life before returning back to earth. Well that's not what happened. What happened was, I thought!

I knew that contradiction was not the hallmark of truth but of falsehood. I knew that God was not a liar and that His word was true. That was a conviction that never left me during this whole arduous process. But what I came to understand was that there was a way to reconcile all of these statements in Scripture and make sense of them. The remedy came by understanding a simple concept—something I had been taught in school in an English class; the difference between the prescriptive and the descriptive.

"What? You are telling me that the enemy was put to flight through an English class. That doesn't sound too spiritual to me."

Well, maybe so, but the truth became clear to me when I understand that there were two ways of looking at the statements mentioned above. One way left me in great confusion, the other way brought everything into clarity.

The first set of Scriptures clearly teach that the one who believes has eternal life... whoever calls on the name of the Lord will be saved... and so on...

The second set of Scriptures outline the need to persevere, to continue in faith. These could be viewed as prescriptive (they tell us to do something) OR they could be viewed as descriptive (they describe actions being done). When seen as *descriptive*, all of them make sense.

Here's what I mean. Let's take the Scripture "the one who endures to the end will be saved." (Matt. 24:13). We could interpret this as saying, "Well, you never can have full assurance of salvation unless you first endure to the end. Case closed. No one can ever have assurance."

That is one way to read the words and many in fact interpret the verse that way. However, that understanding would set itself in total opposition against an entire book of the Bible, namely

First John. John wrote "I have written these things to you that you might know that you have eternal life." (1 John 5:13). John (and of course God, who inspired the words) wrote to make his readers assured of their salvation.

So again which was it? Is it "no one can know" or "God wants us to know"? The fact that God wants us to know we are saved is a clear statement of Scripture. There is no other way to understand the words. So the way to reconcile both statements became clear to me. The verses that teach the need to endure to the end are descriptive rather than prescriptive. A true Christian NEEDS to endure. In fact, he MUST endure — all the way to the end. But here's the truth that helped me so much: SAVING FAITH ENDURES.

This demonstrates that true, saving faith is supernatural in origin. The true Christian WILL endure. Matthew is describing the character trait of the true saint, namely endurance. If you see someone endure to the end, it is the evidence of the fact that they are a truly saved individual. The one enduring is a saved person.

The Apostle John made it clear that those who do not continue in the faith were never truly genuine disciples. 1 John 2:19 reads, "They went out from us, but they were not of us; for if they had been of us, they would have continued with us. But they went out, that it might become plain that they all are not of us." Once again we see that the true Christian WILL endure—the enduring one is a saved person.

Oh how this helped me! I could then see that there is a false kind of faith that looks a lot like the real thing but, in fact, is not genuine. Those who have this kind of "faith" will not last—they endure for a while, but when pressures of life and the cares of this world come, they fall away.

Doesn't that sound a lot like one of Jesus' parables? Yes, exactly!—the Parable of the Sower. (Matt. 13, Mark 4).Those who have the word planted in the soil of the heart do endure. Endure they must and endure they will!

"But wait!" someone might say, "You haven't yet endured to the end, so how can you be sure you will?"

Oh that comes back to the first thing I mentioned in the chapter; the settled peace that the Holy Spirit gave me when I first came to Christ. He gave me the assurance that I belonged to God, and now asks me to examine myself to see if I am in the faith—asking myself questions such as, "Are you still enduring, even in troubled times?" The answer is "yes"—and the good news is that because He is the Source of my faith (it is not the product of my own fleshly carnal unregenerate nature) ... because it is He who started this work in me, I can be confident of this—He who started the work will carry it through to completion.

"But what about holiness John—are you as holy as you should be?"

Well I have to admit, God's standards are perfect, and I come short of the mark each and every day I live.

"Well then John, does that not mean that you can have no real assurance of salvation?"

No, not at all, because I do sense some holiness, I do see growth in sanctification, being set apart to God. But my standing with God is based on being justified by grace alone through faith alone in Christ alone (1), and the wonderful truth is that Christ Himself IS my sanctification. Though the process has certainly begun in me of making me more like Him (even though many times I still fail to honor the Lord as I should), progress is being made. I do want to be holy. I do wish to live free from sin. Yet my standing in holiness is the very holiness of Christ. (2)

"And because of him you are in Christ Jesus, who became to us wisdom from God, righteousness and SANCTIFICATION and redemption, so that, as it is written, "Let the one who boasts, boast in the Lord." (1 Cor. 1:30, 31—emphasis mine)

My sincere prayer is this. "Lord, make me more like You, help me to hate my sin more each day and love Your ways instead, and draw me closer to You, not to try and gain salvation by my works, but because I am a saved man, wanting, desiring, longing for more of You."

The saved man endures, strives, presses and perseveres. He must do so, and he will do so. Why? Because I am confident of this very thing—that the One who has begin the work in me He will perform it until the day of Jesus Christ. None of His true sheep will be lost. Hallelujah, what a Shepherd. Hallelujah, what a Savior!"

———————

(1) *"Justification by grace alone through faith alone because of Christ alone does not lead to more sinning. On the contrary, it is the only sure and hopeful base of operations from which the fight against sin can be launched. All the bombers that go out to drop bombs on the strongholds of sin remaining in our lives take off from the runway of justification by faith alone. The missiles that we shoot against the incoming attack of temptation are launched from the base of justification by faith alone. The whole lifelong triumphant offensive called "operation sanctification"—by which we wage war against all the remaining corruption in our lives—is sustained by the supply*

line of the Spirit that comes from the secure, unassailable home-base of justification by faith alone. And it will be a successful operation—but only because of the unassailable home base."—Dr. John Piper (Sermon, How We Come to Know Sin, Romans 7:7–12, desiringgod.org)

(2) In Scripture, holiness is not primarily about behavior but about being set apart to God's ownership and His service. To be holy is to belong to God; uniquely set apart to Him. God declares His people as positionally holy by virtue of the Person and work of Christ (Col. 1:2). Hebrews 10:10 says, "And by that will we have been sanctified through the offering of the body of Jesus Christ once for all." Then, having declared us holy, God sets about the task of making us holy, shaping our character to become more and more conformed to the image of Christ. This aspect of holiness is a matter of progressively becoming in practice what we already are positionally in Christ. Hebrews 12:10—"For they disciplined us for a short time as it seemed best to them, but he disciplines us for our good, that we may share his holiness."

CHAPTER 19

SPIRITUAL DYSLEXIA

Dyslexia warps reality; the consequences of which can be catastrophic. It is something that causes great hardship to multitudes in our day. People with normal, or even above normal, intelligence suffer from dyslexia as the brain reverses numbers, letters or words. It is a huge learning handicap and, in severe cases, can greatly limit education and employment opportunities.

For those unfamiliar with the problem, imagine having the word "GOD" written clearly in front of you and yet your brain interprets the information as "DOG," as the first and last letters of the word are transposed. I am sure you will agree that there is a vast chasm of difference inherent in this misinterpretation. My heart truly goes out to those who have to go through life having to combat dyslexia.

Moving from the physical to the spiritual realm, I believe multitudes of Christians suffer from what I would call "spiritual dyslexia." It's a phrase I heard some years ago and found it to be a striking one. Theologians don't use this language of course. They would be much more comfortable describing this concept as "the noetic effects of sin," which is the simple recognition that since the Fall of Adam, all of mankind's faculties have been negatively affected, including his mind. In simple terms, we just don't think now as clearly and precisely as we would have done if there had been no Fall.

According to 1 Corinthians 13, this side of glory, we only see through a glass darkly. One day, we will all comprehend things exactly (as much as finite minds can grasp the infinite). Yet right now, we all have our traditions and blind spots. If we knew exactly where we were wrong, we would change our viewpoint immediately. But the point is that we do not see these things until God the Holy Spirit enlightens us and overcomes the effects of our depravity.

Someone suffering with spiritual dyslexia then reads certain Bible verses and, though the words are clear, the traditions of men jumble up the words or miss key words entirely in a sentence. Or they just do not grasp the meaning at all. I speak here from my own experience, as I can honestly say that I had read certain verses a certain way (giving them what I believed to be a true interpretation) for many years until, suddenly, God the Holy Spirit allowed me to overcome my deeply ingrained spiritual dyslexia to see what the Scripture actually said. This is especially true in my own theological journey towards Reformed theology. I say this (hopefully) not out of spiritual pride, but simply out of sincere grateful thanks to God for opening up my understanding to the true nature of His grace. Please allow me to cite just a few examples of what I am referring to with a few quotes from the Gospel of John.

As I have mentioned before, in John chapter 3, Jesus made it clear that unless one is born again he cannot see (or enter) the kingdom of God. (John 3:3, 5).

I understood correctly that people enter the kingdom of God by faith. But my spiritual dyslexia would not allow me see the clear meaning of the words of Christ. Jesus said that only born again people could enter. My tradition said that if I exercised faith I would enter the kingdom and be born again. The problem with this view though is that it has non-born again people entering the kingdom—something that Jesus said was impossible. Such a concept reverses Jesus' words. Unless someone is born again (first) he cannot enter. Therefore, regeneration precedes faith.

This is not the only place in Scripture that teaches this. The verb tenses of the original Greek of 1 John 5:1 reveal that the one going on (present continuous action) believing in Christ has already been born of God. The believing is evidence of regeneration, not the other way round. This is, of course, in perfect harmony with Jesus' clear words in John 3.

Another example is John 6:37, which is again a text already mentioned in this book. Here Jesus makes the statement that "All that the Father gives me will come to me..."

The context here is that Jesus is addressing a crowd of people who, in His words, do not believe in Him (v. 36). He then explains their unbelief, starting with the verse in focus now.

For many years, I would see these words but interpret them through the lens of my tradition, which said that God, being omniscient and knowing the future ahead of time, foresaw those who would come to Christ, and that all in this group were then given as a gift by the Father to the Son. Such was my spiritual dyslexia! I had reversed Jesus' clear words.

To see this, let us ask this question as we look once again at the text. Which came first: the people coming, or the Father giving?

Clearly, it is the Father's giving that comes first. In explaining the unbelief of the crowd in front of Him, Jesus teaches us that the Father gives a certain group of people to the Son, who will then (in time) come to the Son.

My tradition reversed the order of the text, believing it was the peoples' coming to the Son that prompted the Father's giving of that people to the Son. But Jesus taught that everyone who is first given by the Father to the Son will indeed come to the Son.

The final passage I will quote to show how spiritual dyslexia can affect us is John 10:25,26. Once again, Jesus is addressing a crowd of unbelievers and says, "I told you, and you do not believe. The works that I do in my Father's name bear witness about me, but you do not believe because you are not part of my flock."

For many years, I read this last statement of Christ but did not grasp what it actually said. Instead, I interpreted it through the lens of my tradition, which said that people could choose to be part of Christ's flock. In other words, if someone is not part of Christ's flock, they can simply choose to be—their believing will make them one of Christ's sheep. But this is the exact opposite of what Jesus said. Jesus looks people right in the face, telling them that the reason they do not believe is because they are not part of His flock. Once again, my tradition reversed Jesus words completely. Jesus said, "You do not believe because you are not part of my flock."

Of course, neither I nor anyone else has a right to reverse Jesus' words. As a disciple of Christ, my role is to allow Him to be the Lord over my thinking and to come to His word and allow any tradition I have to be either confirmed by His word, or else refuted by His word. It takes courage sometimes to allow traditions to be exposed to the light of Scripture, but once a tradition is seen to be in opposition to the truth of Scripture, I have no business holding on to my tradition. Let God be true and every man (and tradition) a liar.

I came to embrace Reformed theology not because of a love for some theological system but because I love and revere God's word and find that the Bible teaches the doctrines of grace. I also came to see that my traditional interpretation of Scripture was nothing less than spiritual dyslexia.

I still have my blind spots, of course (and if I could see them, they would no longer be blind spots), but I am so thankful to God for the light He has shown me that stresses the graciousness of His grace.

May I challenge each of us to look again at the words of Christ? If you, like me, find that you have reversed Jesus' clear words, I ask you to have the courage to renounce your tradition and embrace the doctrine of Christ. My continued prayer for both myself and all who read these words is that God will lead and guide us into the truth of His Word.

CHAPTER 20

AS THE KING'S HERALD

I stand before you today as the King's herald with a message of supreme importance. This King I serve is the Creator of all things. He has made you for Himself, giving you life and all the blessings of His gracious hand.

Yet all mankind are rebels at heart, violating His laws with reckless abandon. Every sin we commit is an act of high treason defying His right of ownership and His holy character. Being a just and holy King, He must dispense justice to all perpetrators. These acts, being as traitorous as they are, deserve His wrath in full measure. He has every right to sentence all rebels to eternal punishment while also wiping them off the face of the earth.

Yet, this Great King, moved by love and as a display of vast mercy, has sent His dearly loved Son into the world, to live a righteous life, and at the cross, bear the punishment and guilt of all those who would believe in Him. So, to all who would renounce all attempts of self-justification, and who will take refuge in Jesus Christ, the Son of God, this King announces that He will forgive all your treasonous acts, on the basis that His own Son was punished in your place, and instead, He will transfer the righteousness of His Son to your account so that you stand before Him guiltless and righteous in His sight. For He who knew no sin was made to be sin for us, so that in Him we might be made the righteousness of God.

So to all who take refuge in the Son, you need not face the King's fierce and holy wrath; only trust in, believe in the Lord Jesus Christ, the resurrected Savior, now enthroned in the courts of heaven.

This is the good news I have been sent to proclaim as His herald.

John Chapter 3, verse 36 says, "Whoever believes in the Son has eternal life; whoever does not obey the Son shall not see life, but the wrath of God remains on him."

All rebels of the King, hear the word of the Lord. Repent of both your treason and all your vain attempts to please Him. Trust in the Son. Trust in His finished work upon the cross. Come to Him now. Make Him your refuge, and the King extends to you full pardon for all your acts of high treason, and a place with Him at His banqueting table where you will enjoy the King's favor and bounty always. In His presence there is fullness of joy and at His right hand there are pleasures forevermore.

Yet this free offer of good news will not last forever. Come to Him for now indeed is the day of salvation. Call upon the Name of the Lord and be saved!

FURTHER RECOMMENDED RESOURCES:

BOOKS:
Whatever Happened to the Gospel of Grace? by James
Montgomery Boice

The Doctrines of Grace by James Montgomery Boice

Chosen for Life by Sam Storms

Chosen by God by R C Sproul

Loved by God by R C Sproul

What is Reformed Theology? by R C Sproul

The Potter's Freedom by James R. White

Finally Alive by John Piper

Foundations of Grace by Steven Lawson

Pillars of Grace by Steven Lawson

Putting Amazing Back into Grace by Michael Horton

By Grace Alone by Jim McClarty

The Christian Faith by Michael Horton

Systematic Theology by Wayne Grudem

INTERNET SITES:

monergism.com

reformationtheology.com

effectualgrace.com

salvationbygrace.org

aomin.org

Other Titles by Solid Ground

In addition to *Twelve What Abouts*, we are delighted to offer several titles to help you understand the Doctrines of Grace.

Notes on Galatians by Machen is a reprint that is long overdue, especially in light of the present-day battle of the doctrine articulated in Galatians.

The Origin of Paul's Religion by Machen penetrates to the heart of the matter and speaks to many of the contemporary attacks upon the purity of the Gospel of Christ.

Biblical and Theological Studies by the professors of Princeton in 1912, at the centenary celebration of the Seminary. Articles are by men like Allis, Vos, Warfield, Machen, Wilson and others.

Theology on Fire: Vols. 1 & 2 by J.A. Alexander is the two volumes of sermons by this brilliant scholar from Princeton Seminary.

A Shepherd's Heart by J.W. Alexander is a volume of outstanding expository sermons from the pastoral ministry of one of the leading preachers of the 19th century.

Evangelical Truth by Archibald Alexander is a volume of practical sermons intended to be used for Family Worship.

The Lord of Glory by B.B. Warfield is one of the best treatments of the doctrine of the Deity of Christ ever written. Warfield is simply masterful.

The Power of God unto Salvation by B.B. Warfield is the first book of sermons ever published of this master-theologian. Several of these are found nowhere else.

The Person & Work of the Holy Spirit by B.B. Warfield is a compilation of all the sermons, articles and book reviews by a master-theologian on a theme that should interest every child of God. Brilliant in every way!

Grace & Glory by Geerhardus Vos is a series of addresses delivered in the chapel to the students at Princeton. John Murray said of him, "Dr. Vos is, in my judgment, the most penetrating exegete it has been my privilege to know, and I believe, the most incisive exegete that has appeared in the English-speaking world in this century."

Princeton Sermons: *Chapel Addresses from 1891-92* by B.B. Warfield, W.H. Green, C.W. Hodge, John D. Davis and More. According to Joel Beeke, this is "a treasure-trove of practical Christianity delivered by some of the greatest preachers and seminary teachers America has ever known."

Call us at **1-205-443-0311**
Send us an e-mail at **mike.sgcb@gmail.com**
Visit us on line at **www.solid-ground-books.com**

CPSIA information can be obtained at www.ICGtesting.com
Printed in the USA
LVOW060144230312

274429LV00002B/2/P